Thoughts I Met On the Highway
and other truths

Thoughts I Met On the Highway and Other Truths
By Ralph Waldo Trine

Start Publishing PD LLC
Copyright © 2024 by Start Publishing PD LLC

All rights reserved, including the right to reproduce this book or portions thereof in any form whatsoever.

Start Publishing PD is a registered trademark of Start Publishing PD LLC
Manufactured in the United States of America

Cover art: Shutterstock/Taisiya Kozorez

Cover design: Jennifer Do

10 9 8 7 6 5 4 3 2 1

ISBN 979-8-8809-2353-3

Table of Contents

Thoughts I Met On the Highway 6
A Creed of the Open Road 23
The Greatest Thing Ever Known 47

Thoughts I Met On the Highway

Thoughts are forces—like builds like and like attracts like. Thoughts of strength both build strength from within and attract it from without. Thoughts of weakness actualize weakness from within and attract it from without. Courage begets strength, fear begets weakness. And so courage begets success, fear begets failure.

Any way the old world goes
Happy be the weather!
With the red thorn or the rose
Singin' all together!
Don't you see that sky o' blue!
Good Lord painted it for you

Reap the daisies in the dew
Singin' all together!
Springtime sweet, an' frosty fall
Happy be the weather!
Earth has gardens for us all,
Goin' on together.

Sweet the labor in the light,
To the harvest's gold and white—
Till the toilers say "Good night,"
Singin' all together!

There is no quality that exerts more good, is of greater service to all mankind during the course of the ordinary life, than the mind and the heart that goes out in an all-embracing love for all, that is the generator and the circulator of a genuine, hearty, wholesome sympathy and courage and good cheer, that is not disturbed or upset by the passing occurrence little or great, but that is serene, tranquil, and conquering to the end, that is looking for the best, that is finding the best, and that is inspiring the best in all. There is moreover, no quality that when genuine brings such rich returns to its possessor by virtue of the thoughts and the feelings that it inspires and calls forth from others and that come back laden with their peaceful, stimulating, healthful influences for you.

Thoughts I Met On the Highway

Out of the night that covers me,
Black as the Pit from pole to pole,
I thank whatever gods may be
For my unconquerable soul.

In the fell clutch of circumstance
I have not winced nor cried aloud.
Under the bludgeoning of chance
My head is bloody, but unbowed.

Beyond this place of wrath and tears
Looms but the horror of the shade,
And yet the menace of the years
Finds and shall find me, unafraid.

It matters not how strait the gate
How charged with punishment the scroll,
I am the master of my fate;
I am the captain of my soul.—*William Earnest Henley*

Thought is the great builder in human life: it is the determining factor. Continually think thoughts that are good, and your life will show forth in goodness, and your body in health and beauty. Continually think evil thoughts, and your life will show forth in evil, and your body in weakness and repulsiveness. Think thoughts of love, and you will love and will be loved. Think thoughts of hatred, and you will hate and will be hated. Each follows its kind.

Every day is a fresh beginning,
Every morning is the world made new;
You who are weary of sorrow and sinning,
Here is a beautiful hope for you,
A hope for me and a hope for you.

All the past things are past and over,
The tasks are done, and the tears are shed.
Yesterday's errors let yesterday cover;
Yesterday's wounds, which smarted and bled,

Are healed with the healing which night has shed.

Every day is a fresh beginning,
Listen, my soul, to the glad refrain,
And, spite of old sorrow and older sinning,
And puzzles forecasted, and possible pain,
Take heart with the day and begin again.

Each morning is a fresh beginning. We are, as it were, just beginning life. We have it *entirely* in our own hands. And when the morning with its fresh beginning comes, all yesterdays should be yesterdays, with which we have nothing to do. Sufficient is it to know that the way we lived our yesterday has determined for us our today. And, again, when the morning with its fresh beginning comes, all tomorrows should be tomorrows, with which we have nothing to do. Sufficient to know that the way we live our today determines our tomorrow.

Simply the first hour of this new day, with all its richness and glory, with all its sublime and eternity-determining possibilities, and each succeeding hour as it comes, but *not before* it comes—this is the secret of character building. This simple method will bring any one to the realization of the highest life that can be even conceived of, and there is nothing in this connection that can be conceived of that cannot be realized somehow, somewhen, somewhere.

The poem hangs on the berry-bush
When comes the poet's eye,
And the whole street is a masquerade
When Shakespeare passes by.

This same Shakespeare, whose mere passing causes all this commotion, is the one who put into the mouth of one of his creations the words: "The fault, dear Brutus, is not in our stars, but in ourselves, that we are underlings." And again he gave us a great truth when he said:

"Our doubts are traitors,
And make us lose the good we oft might win
By fearing to attempt."

Thoughts I Met On the Highway

There is probably no agent that brings us more undesirable conditions than fear. We should live in fear of nothing, nor will we when we come fully to know ourselves. An old French proverb runs:

"Some of your griefs you have cured,
And the sharpest you still have survived;
But what torments of pain you endured
From evils that never arrived."

Fear and lack of faith go hand in hand. The one is born of the other. Tell me how much one is given to fear, and I will tell you how much he lacks in faith. Fear is a most expensive guest to entertain, the same as worry is: so expensive are they that no one can afford to entertain them. We invite what we fear, the same as, by a different attitude of mind, we invite and attract the influences and conditions we desire.

To remain in nature always sweet and simple and humble, and therefore strong.

"Whatever the weather may be," says he,
"Whatever the weather may be,
It's the songs ye sing, an' the smiles ye wear,
That's a-makin' the sun shine everywhere."—*James Whitcomb Riley*

Sweetness of nature, simplicity in manners and conduct, humility without self-abasement, give the truly kingly quality to men, the queenly to women, the winning to children, whatever the rank or the station may be. The life dominated by this characteristic, or rather these closely allied characteristics, is a natural well-spring of joy to itself and sheds a continual benediction upon all who come within the scope of its influence. It makes for a life of great beauty in itself, and it imparts courage and hope and buoyancy to all others.

There is no thing we cannot overcome;
Say not thy evil instinct is inherited,
Or that some trait inborn makes thy whole life forlorn;
And calls down punishment that is not merited.

Back of thy parents and grandparents lies
The Great Eternal Will! That too is thine
Inheritance,—strong, beautiful, divine,
Sure lever of success for one who tries.

Earth has no claim the soul cannot contest;
Know thyself part of the Eternal Source;
Naught can stand before thy spirit's force:
The soul's Divine Inheritance is best.

Thought is at the bottom of all progress or retrogression, of all success or failure, of all that is desirable or undesirable in human life. The type of thought we entertain both creates and draws conditions that crystallize about it, conditions exactly the same in nature as is the thought that gives them form. Thoughts are forces, and each creates of its kind, whether we realize it or not. The great law of the drawing power of the mind, which says that like creates like, and that like attracts like, is continually working in every human life, for it is one of the great immutable laws of the universe. For one to take time to see clearly the things one would attain to, and then to hold that ideal steadily and continually before his mind, never allowing faith—his positive thought-forces—to give way to or to be neutralized by doubts and fears, and then to set about doing each day what his hands find to do, never complaining, but spending the time that he would otherwise spend in complaint in focusing his thought-forces upon the ideal that his mind has built, will sooner or later bring about the full materialization of that for which he sets out.

Beauty seen is never lost,
God's colors all are fast;
The glory of this sunset heaven
Into my soul has passed,—
A sense of gladness unconfined
To mortal, date or clime;
As the soul liveth, it shall live
Beyond the years of time.
Beside the mystic asphodels
Shall bloom the home-born flowers,

And new horizons flush and glow
With sunset hues of ours. —*Whittier*

Would you remain always young, and would you carry all the joyousness and buoyancy of youth into your maturer years? Then have care concerning but one thing,—how you live in your thought world. It was the inspired one, Gautama, the Buddha, who said,—"The mind is everything; what you think you become." And the same thing had Ruskin in mind when he said,—"Make yourselves nests of pleasant thoughts. None of us as yet know, for none of us have been taught in early youth, what fairy palaces we may build of beautiful thought—*proof against all adversity*." And would you have in your body all the elasticity, all the strength, all the beauty of your younger years? Then live these in your mind, making no room for unclean thought, and you will externalize them in your body. In the degree that you keep young in thought will you remain young in body. And you will find that your body will in turn aid your mind, for body helps mind the same as mind helps body.

There is a sacred Something on all ways—
Something that watches through the Universe;
One that remembers, reckons and repays,
Giving us love for love, and curse for curse. —*Edwin Markham*

The power of every life, the very life itself, is determined by what it relates itself to. God is immanent as well as transcendent. He is creating, working, ruling in the universe today, in your life and in mine, just as much as He ever has been. We are too apt to regard Him after the manner of an absentee landlord, one who has set in operation the forces of this great universe, and then taken Himself away.

In the degree, however, that we recognize Him as immanent as well as transcendent, are we able to partake of His life and power. For in the degree that we recognize Him as the Infinite Spirit of Life and Power that is today, at this very moment, working and manifesting in and through all, and then, in the degree that we come into the realization of our oneness with this life, do we become partakers of, and so do we actualize in ourselves the qualities of his life. In the degree that we open ourselves to the inflowing tide of this immanent and transcendent life, do we make ourselves channels through which the Infinite Intelligence and Power can work.

> The robber is robbed by his riches;
> The tyrant is dragged by his chain;
> The schemer is snared by his cunning,
> The slayer lies dead by the slain.—*Edwin Markham*

This is the law of prosperity: When apparent adversity comes, be not cast down by it, but make the best of it, and always look forward for better things, for conditions more prosperous. To hold yourself in this attitude of mind is to set into operation subtle, silent, and irresistible forces that sooner or later will actualize in material form that which is today merely an idea. But ideas have occult power, and ideas, when rightly planted and rightly tended, are the seeds that actualize material conditions.

Never give a moment to complain, but utilize the time that would otherwise be spent in this way in looking forward and actualizing the conditions you desire. Suggest prosperity to yourself. See yourself in a prosperous condition. Affirm that you will before long be in a prosperous condition. Affirm it calmly and quietly, but strongly and confidently. Believe it, believe it absolutely. Expect it,—keep it continually watered with expectation. You thus make yourself a magnet to attract the things that you desire. Don't be afraid to suggest.

> They might not need me—yet they might,
> I'll let my heart be just in sight.
> A smile so small as mine might be
> Precisely their necessity. —*Emily Dickinson*

The grander natures and the more thoughtful are always looking for and in conversation dwelling on the better things in others. It is the rule with but few, if any exceptions, that the more noble and worthy and thoughtful the nature, the more it is continually looking for the best there is to be found in every life. Instead of judging or condemning, or acquiring the habit that eventually leads to this, it is looking more closely to and giving its time to living more worthily itself.

Thoughts I Met On the Highway

It is in this way continually unfolding and expanding in beauty and in power; it is finding an ever-increasing happiness by the admiration and the love that such a life is always, even though all unconsciously, calling to itself from all sources. It is the life that pays by many fold.

> We just shake hands at meeting
> With many that come nigh
> We nod the head in greeting
> To many that go by—
>
> But welcome through the gateway
> Our few old friends and true;
> Then hearts leap up, and straightway
> There's open house for you.
> Old friends.
> There's open house for you! —*Gerald Massey*

Many times the struggles are greater than we can ever know. We need more gentleness and sympathy and compassion in our common human life. Then we will neither blame nor condemn. Instead of blaming or condemning we will sympathize.

> "Comfort one another.
> For the way is often dreary
> And the feet are often weary,
> And the heart is very sad.
> There is a heavy burden bearing,
> When it seems that none are caring,
> And we half forget that ever we were glad.
>
> "Comfort one another
> With the hand-clasp close and tender.
> With the sweetness love can render,
> And the looks of friendly eyes.
> Do not wait with grace unspoken,
> While life's daily bread is broken—
> Gentle speech is oft like manna from the skies."

And then when we fully realize the fact that selfishness is at the root of all error, sin, and crime, and that ignorance is the basis of all selfishness, with what charity we come to look upon the acts of all. It is the ignorant man who seeks his own ends at the expense of the greater whole. It is the ignorant man, therefore, who is the selfish man.

To get up immediately when we stumble, face again to the light, and travel on without wasting even a moment in regret.

We are on the way from the imperfect to the perfect; some day, in this life or some other, we shall reach our destiny. It is as much the part of folly to waste time and cripple our forces in vain, unproductive regrets in regard to the occurences of the past as it is to cripple our forces through fears and forebodings for the future.

There is no experience in any life which if rightly recognized, rightly turned and thereby wisely used, cannot be made of value; many times things thus turned and used can be made sources of inestimable gain; ofttimes they become veritable blessings in disguise.

'Tis the sweetest thing to remember
If courage be on the wane.
When the cold, dark days are over—
Why, the birds go north again.—*Ella Higginson*

Nothing is more subtle than thought, nothing more powerful, nothing more irresistible in its operations, when rightly applied and held to with a faith and fidelity that is unswerving,—a faith and fidelity that never knows the neutralizing effects of doubt and fear. If one have aspirations and a sincere desire for a higher and better condition, so far as advantages, facilities, associates, or any surroundings or environments are concerned, and if he continually send out his highest thought forces for the realization of these desires, and continually water these forces with firm expectation as to their fulfillment, he will sooner or later find himself in the realization of these desires, and all in accordance with natural laws and forces.

We are born to be neither slaves nor beggars, but to dominion and to plenty. This is our rightful heritage, if we will but recognize and lay claim to it.

Thoughts I Met On the Highway

> One who never turned his back, but marched breast forward,
> Never doubted clouds would break,
> Never dreamed, though right were worsted, wrong would triumph,
> Held we fall to rise, are baffled to fight better,
> Sleep to wake.—*Robert Browning*

Will is the steady directing power: it is concentration. It is the pilot which, after the vessel is started by the mighty force within, puts it on its right course and keeps it true to that course.

Will is the sun-glass which so concentrates and so focuses the sun's rays that they quickly burn a hole through the paper that is held before it. The same rays, not thus concentrated, not thus focused, would fall upon the paper for days without any effect whatever. Will is the means for the directing, the concentrating, the focusing, of the thought-forces. Thought under wise direction,—this it is that does the work, that brings results, that makes the successful career. One object in mind which we never lose sight of; an ideal steadily held before the mind, never lost sight of, never lowered, never swerved from,—this, with *persistence*, determines all. Nothing can resist the power of thought, when thus directed by will.

> To stand by one's friend to the uttermost end,
> And fight a fair fight with one's foe;
> Never to quit and never to twit,
> And never to peddle one's woe. —*George Brinton Chandler*

The fearing, grumbling, worrying, vascillating do not succeed in anything and generally live by burdening, in some form or another, someone else. They stand in the way of, they prevent their own success; they fail in living even an ordinary healthy, normal life; they cast a blighting influence over and they act as a hindrance to all with whom they at any time come in contact. The pleasures we take captive in life, the growth and advancement we make, the pleasure and benefit our company or acquaintanceship brings to others, the very desirability of our companionship on the part of others—all depend upon the types of thought we entertain and live most habitually with.

No one could tell me where my Soul might be.
I searched for God but God eluded me.
I sought my brother out and found all there.—*Ernest Crosby*.

In the degree that we love will we be loved. Thoughts are forces. Each creates of its kind. Each comes back laden with the effect that corresponds to itself and of which it is the cause.

"Then let your secret thoughts be fair—
They have a vital part, and share
In shaping words and moulding fate;
God's system is so intricate."

If our heart goes out in love to all with whom we come in contact, we inspire love and the same ennobling and warming influences of love always return to us from those in whom we inspire them. There is a deep scientific principle underlying the precept—If you would have all the world love you, you must first love all the world.

It was only a glad "Good morning!"
As she passed along the way,
But it spread the morning glory
Over the livelong day.

By example and not by precept. By living, not by preaching. By doing, not by professing. By living the life, not by dogmatizing as to how it should be lived. There is no contagion equal to the contagion of life. Whatever we sow, that shall we also reap, and each thing sown produces of its kind. We can kill not only by doing another bodily injury directly, but we can and we do kill by every antagonistic thought. Not only do we thus kill, but while we kill we suicide. Many a man has been made sick by having the ill thoughts of a number of people centered upon him; some have been actually killed. Put hatred into the world and we make it a literal hell. Put love into the world and heaven with all its beauties and glories becomes a reality.

Not to love is not to live, or it is to live a living death. The life that goes out in love to all is the life that is full, and rich, and continually expanding in beauty and in power. Such is the life that becomes ever more inclusive, and hence larger in its scope and influence.

> Give us men!
> Strong and stalwart ones:
> Men whom highest hope inspires,
> Men whom purest honour fires,
> Men who trample Self beneath them.
> Men who make their country wreathe them
> As her noble sons,
> Worthy of their sires,
> Men who never shame their mothers,
> Men who never fail their brothers,
> True, however false are others:
> Give us Men—I say again,
> Give us Men!—*The Bishop of Exeter*

Not repression, but elevation. Would that this could be repeated a thousand times over! *No, a knowledge of the spiritual realities of life prohibits asceticism, repression, the same as it prohibits license and perverted use. To err on the one side is just as contrary to the ideal life as to err on the other.* All things are for a purpose, all should be used and enjoyed; but all should be rightly used, that they may be fully enjoyed.

It is the all-around, fully developed we want,—not the ethereal, pale-blooded man and woman, but the man and woman of flesh and blood, for action and service here and now,—the man and woman strong and powerful, with all the faculties and functions fully unfolded and used, all in a royal and bounding condition, but all rightly subordinated. The man and the woman of this kind, with the imperial hand of mastery upon all,—standing, moving thus like a king, nay, like a very God,—such is the man and such is the woman of power. Such is the ideal life: anything else is one-sided, and falls short of it.

> High thought and noble in all lands
> Help me; my soul is fed by such,
> But oh, at the touch of life and hands—
> The human touch!
> Warm, vital, close, life's Symbol dear,—

These need I most, and now and here.—*Richard Burton*

Thoughts of strength both build strength from within and attract it from without. Thoughts of weakness actualize weakness from within and attract it from without. Courage begets strength, fear begets weakness. And so courage begets success, fear begets failure. It is the man or the woman of faith, and hence of courage, who is the master of circumstances, and who make his or her power felt in the world. It is the man or the woman who lacks faith and who as a consequence is weakened and crippled by fears and forebodings, who is the creature of all passing occurences.

What one lives in his invisible thought world he is continually actualizing in his visible material world. If he would have any conditions different in the latter he must make the necessary change in the former. A clear realization of this great fact would bring success to thousands of men and women who all about us are now in the depths of despair. It would bring health, abounding health and strength to thousands now diseased and suffering. It would bring peace and joy to thousands now unhappy and ill at ease.

> I stay my haste, I make delays,
> For what avails this eager pace?
> I stand amid eternal ways,
> And what is mine shall know my face
>
> Asleep, awake, by night or day,
> The friends I seek are seeking me;
> No wind can drive my bark astray,
> Nor change the tide of destiny—
>
> The waters know their own, and draw
> The brooks that spring in yonder height;
> So flows the good with equal law
> Unto the soul of pure delight.
>
> The stars come nightly to the sky;
> The tidal wave unto the sea;
> Nor time, nor space, nor deep, nor high,
> Can keep my own away from me.—*John Burroughs*

The thing that pays, and that makes for a well balanced, useful, and happy life, is not necessarily and is not generally a somber, pious morality, or any standard of life that keeps us from a free, happy, spontaneous use and enjoyment of all normal and healthy faculties, functions, and powers, the enjoyment of all innocent pleasures—use, but not abuse, enjoyment, but enjoyment through self-mastery and not through license or perverted use, for it can never come that way. Look where we will, in or out and around us, we will find that it is the middle ground—neither poverty nor excessive riches, good wholesome use without license, a turning into the bye-ways along the main road where innocent and healthy God-sent and God-intended pleasures and enjoyments are to be found; but never getting far enough away to lose sight of the road itself. The middle ground it is that the wise man or woman plants foot upon.

> For evil poisons; malice shafts
> Like boomerangs return,
> Inflicting wounds that will not heal
> While rage and anger burn.

Tell me how much one loves and I will tell you how much he has seen of God. Tell me how much he loves and I will tell you how much he lives with God. Tell me how much he loves and I will tell you how far into the Kingdom of Heaven,—the kingdom of harmony, he has entered, for "love is the fulfilling of the law."

And in a sense love is everything. It is the key to life, and its influences are those that move the world. Live only in the thought of love for all and you will draw love to you from all. Live in the thought of malice or hatred, and malice and hatred will come back to you.

And so love inspires love; hatred breeds hatred. Love and good will stimulate and build up the body; hatred and malice corrode and tear it down. Love is a savor of life unto life; hatred is a savor of death unto death.

> "There are loyal hearts, there are spirits brave,
> There are souls that are pure and true;
> Then give to the world the best you have,
> And the best will come back to you.

"Give love, and love to *your* heart will flow,
A strength in your utmost need;
Have faith, and a score of hearts will show
Their faith in *your* word and deed."

The kind of a man for you and me!
He faces the world unflinchingly,
And smiles as long as the world exists,
With a knuckled faith and force like fists:
He lives the life he is preaching of,
And loves where most is the need of love;
And feeling still, with a grief half glad,
That the bad are as good as the good are bad,
He strikes straight out for the right—and he
Is the kind of a man for you and me!—*James Whitcomb Riley*

After a certain age is reached in any life, the prevailing tone and condition of that life is the resultant of the mental habits of that life. If one have mental equipment sufficient to find and to make use of the Science of Thought in its application to scientific mind and body building, habit and character building, there is little by way of heredity, environment, attainment of which he or she will not be the master.

One thing is very certain—the mental points of view, the mental tendencies and habits at twenty-eight and thirty-eight will have externalized themselves and will have stamped the prevailing conditions of any life at forty-eight and fifty-eight and sixty-eight.

Who puts back into place a fallen bar,
Or flings a rock out of a traveled road,
His feet are moving toward the central star,
His name is whispered in the Gods' abode.—*Edwin Markham*

We need changes from the duties and the cares of our accustomed everyday life. They are necessary for healthy, normal living. We need occasionally to be away from our friends, our relatives, from the members of our immediate households. Such changes are good for us; they are good for them. We appreciate them better, they us, when we are away from them for a period, or they from us.

We need these changes to get the kinks out of our minds, our nerves, our muscles—the cobwebs off our faces. We need them to whet again the edge of appetite. We need them to invite the mind and the soul to new possibilities and powers. We need them in order to come back with new implements, or with implements redressed, sharpened, for the daily duties.

We need periods of being by ourselves—*alone*. Sometimes a fortnight or even a week will do wonders for one, unless he or she has drawn too heavily upon the account. The simple custom, moreover, of taking an hour, or even a half hour, *alone in the quiet*, in the midst of the daily routine of life, would be the source of *inestimable gain* for countless numbers.

> I know not where His islands lift
> Their fronded palms in air;
> I only know I cannot drift
> Beyond His love and care.—*Whittier*

We need more faith in everyday life—faith in the power that works for good, faith in the Infinite God, and hence faith in ourselves created in His image. And however things at times may seem to go, however dark at times appearances may be, the knowledge of the fact that "the Supreme Power has us in its charge as it has the suns and endless systems of worlds in space," will give us the supreme faith that all is well with us, the same as all is well with the world. "Thou wilt keep him in perfect peace whose mind is stayed on Thee."

There is nothing firmer, and safer, and surer than Deity. Then, as we recognize the fact that we have it in our own hands to open ourselves ever more fully to this Infinite Power, and call upon it to manifest itself in and through us, we will find in ourselves an ever increasing sense of power. For in this way we are working in conjunction with it, and it in turn is working in conjunction with us. We are then led into the full realization of the fact that all things work together for good to those that love the good.

> Earth breaks up, time drops away,
> In flows Heaven with its new day.—*Browning*

A Creed of the Open Road

To be observed today, to be changed tomorrow, or abandoned, according to tomorrows light.

To live to our highest in all things that pertain to us, and to lend a hand as best we can to all others for this same end.

To aid in righting the wrongs that cross our path by pointing the wrong-doer to a better way, and thus aid him in becoming a power for good.

To turn toward and to keep our faces always to the light, knowing that we are then always safe, and that we shall travel with joy the open road.

To love the fields and the wild flowers, the stars, the far-open sea, the soft, warm earth, and to live much with them alone; but to love struggling and weary men and women and every pulsing, living creature better.

To do our own thinking, listening quietly to the opinions of others, but to be sufficiently men and women to act always upon our own convictions. To do our duty as we see it, regardless of the opinions of others-seeming gain or loss, temporary blame or praise.

To remain in nature always sweet and simple and humble and therefore strong.

To play the part of neither fool nor knave by attempting to Judge another, but to give that same time to living more worthily ourselves.

To get up immediately when we stumble, face again to the light, and travel on without wasting even a moment in regret.

To love and to hold due reverence for all people and all things, but to stand in awe or fear of nothing save our own wrong doing.

To recognize the good lying at the heart of all people, of all things, waiting for expression all in its own good way and time.

To know that it is the middle ground that brings pleasure and satisfaction, and that excesses have to be paid for always with heavy and sometimes with frightful costs. To know that work, occupation, something definite and useful to do, is one of the established conditions of happiness in life.

To realize always clearly that thoughts are forces, that like creates like and like attracts like, and that to determine one's thinking therefore is to determine his life.

To take and to live always in the attitude of mind that compels gladness, looking for and thus drawing to us continually the best in all people and all things, being thereby the creators of our own good fortunes.

To know that the ever-conscious realization of the essential oneness of each life with the Divine Life is the Greatest of all knowledge, and that to open ourselves as opportune channels for the Divine Power to work in and through us is the open door to the highest attainment, and to the best there is in life.

In brief— to be honest, to be fearless, to be just, joyous, kind. This will make our part in life's great and as yet not fully understood play one of greatest glory, and we need then stand in fear of nothing—life nor death; for death is life. Or rather, it is the quick transition to fife in another form; the putting off of the old coat and the putting on of the new; a passing not from light to darkness, but from light to light according as we have lived here; a taking up of life in another form where we leave it off here; a part in life not to be shunned or dreaded or feared, but to be welcomed with a glad and ready smile when it comes in its own good way and time.

1. To live to our highest in all things that pertain to us, and to lend a hand as best we can to all others for this same end.

Does it pay? Are there any real, substantial reasons that we live to our highest?

The fact that we have ideals and aspirations, and that we always feel better the more fully we follow them, indicates that it pays. That we are conscious that something is not right, and that we suffer when we do violence to that which we know or which we feel to be the better thing, indicates that there is a law written in the universe through the inexorable operation of which we are pushed onward and upward, unless we are wise enough to go of our own accord.

As excessive eating or drinking, as excesses of every nature bring with them something that convinces an ordinarily bright mind that they don't pay, is an indication that there is a law of moderation, the observance of which brings good, the violation of which brings its opposite, pain and loss; as to live in discord with, in hatred or envy or jealousy of one's fellows brings its own peculiar destructive results, indicating that there is a law of love, of kindness, of mutuality, that will admit of no violation without striking home its punishments and inflicting its losses, so the lack of self-respect, the sense of loss, the general feeling that we have missed the higher and the satisfying in pursuing or being contented with the lower and the transient, indicates that the higher, the better, really pays, and that to follow it is a manifestation of simply good everyday common sense.

We shall come to our own sometime, and our own is the highest and best that we know; we shall come by being led in that we voluntarily follow our highest ideals and aspirations, our dreams, if you please, or we shall come by being pushed through suffering and loss and even anguish of soul, until we find all too concretely that the better pays, and more, that it will have obedience.

The thing that pays, and that makes for a well-balanced, useful, and happy life, is not necessarily and is not generally a sombre, pious morality, or any standard of life that keeps us from a free, happy, spontaneous use and enjoyment of all normal and healthy faculties, functions, and powers, the enjoyment of all innocent pleasures — use, but not abuse, enjoyment, but enjoyment through self-mastery and not through license or perverted use, for it can never come that way. Of great suggestive value to us all should be this thought of Thoreau: "Do not be too moral. You may cheat yourself out of much life so. Aim above morality. Be not simply good; be good for something."

As there is, moreover, the great law of love, of service, of mutuality, written at the very core of human life, then in the degree that we are wise we will lend the hand whenever and wherever we can to all others in their strivings for the same life that we find is the better part, and as the influence, the help of example, is greater always than the kind intentions of precept, every strong though struggling life becomes the greatest possible help to every other.

2. To aid in righting the wrongs that cross our path by pointing the wrong-doer to a better way, and thus aid him in becoming a power for good.

Wrongs and injustices of one type or another come to our notice almost daily. They seem worthy of condemnation, many times of punishment. Wise however is he who is able to differentiate between the perpetrator of the wrong and the wrong that is done.

Only he who is perfect himself is in a consistent position even to judge another, to say nothing of condemning. The truly wise therefore will be slow to judge, and he will refuse to condemn. This must ever be so until he who would judge be perfect himself. We are all in the process of attaining — none have yet arrived.

The one whose zeal for justice is so keen can, moreover, rest at least in part peace when he is able once for all to realize that every wrong-doing carries with it its own punishment, that such is a fundamental law, and that by virtue of it the perpetrator of a wrong or an injustice suffers many times more than the one against whom it is directed.

All sin and error, all wrong and injustice, with its attendant suffering and loss, is the result of selfishness. Selfishness is always the result of ignorance — a mind undeveloped or developed only in spots. Therefore to aid in bringing one to a realization of his higher and better self and the laws that operate there, that lie may act and live continually from that center, is after all the effective and the fundamentally common-sense way of aiding in righting the wrongs that help in warping, in crippling, the happiness and the sweetness that belong inherently to every life.

Now and then there is one so steeped in selfishness, so ignorant therefore of the prevailing laws of life, that it is necessary to take the power of oppression or injustice out of his hands, at least for the time being; but the springs of tenderness, of compassion, of love for the right, though sometimes deeply covered or apparently non-existent, can be made in time to burst forth and to overflow by the truly wise, so that even such may in time, as has so often and so abundantly been the case, become one of the noblest, one of the most valuable, of earth's sons or daughters.

When the highest speaks to the highest in another, sooner or later the response is sure. In this way birth is given to ever-widening circles of influence that make for the good, the honest, the righteous, therefore the happy, in this at times hard and complex, but on the whole, good old world of ours.

3. To turn toward and to keep our faces always to the light, knowing that we are then always safe, and that we shall travel with joy the open road.

A nowledge of the fact that we grow into the likeness of those things we contemplate, of those things that we live mostly with in our mental world, is one of the greatest assets of human life. Thought is at the bottom of all progress or retrogression, of all that is desirable or undesirable in life. We have it entirely in our own hands to determine what type of thought we entertain and habitually live with; thereby it is that we are the makers of our own good or ill fortunes.

A knowledge also of the fact that it is not what we actually accomplish at any particular time or times, but what we earnestly endeavor to accomplish, makes the road easier and should make all effort even a joy. It is the law of the reflex nerve system that whenever one does or endeavors to do any given thing in a certain way, a modicum of power is added whereby it is a trifle easier at the next effort, an added trifle at the next and the next, until that which is difficult and is done only with great effort in the beginning becomes easy of accomplishment — that which we do haltingly and stumblingly at first, bye and bye, so to speak, does itself, and with scarcely or even without any conscious effort on our part. This is the law; it is the secret of habit forming, character building, of all attainment.

The first thing then is the earnest desire, which, in other words, is the turning of the face to the light, then the mere traveling on day by day, calmly resting in the assurance that all is well with us now and that this course diligently and calmly pursued will lead us eventually to the sunlit hills and up to and into the very Gates of Paradise.

He who has the quest of the good in his heart has merely to travel on a step at a time, knowing that the second will be made clear when the first is taken. Patience and steadfastness and withal happiness and much laughter, mingled with whatever tears there may be along the way, will make even the most humble life the highest that can be lived. Such a life can end only in triumph; nay, it is a triumph during its progress, and even its failures are parts of its triumph.

4. To love the fields and the wild flowers, the stars, the far-open sea, the soft, warm earth, and to live much with them alone; but to love struggling and weary men and women and every pulsing, living creature better.

Our complex modern life, especially in our larger centers, gets us running so many times into grooves that we are prone to miss, and sometimes for long periods, the all-round, completer life. We are led at times almost to forget that the stars come nightly to the sky, or even that there is a sky; that there are hedgerows and groves where the birds are always singing and where we can lie on our backs and watch the treetops swaying above us and the clouds floating by an hour or hours at a time; where one can live with his soul or, as Whitman has put it, where one can loaf and invite his soul.

We need changes from the duties and the cares of our accustomed everyday life. They are necessary for healthy, normal living. We need occasionally to be away from our friends, our relatives, from the members of our immediate households. Such changes are good for us; they are good for them. We appreciate them better, they us, when we are away from them for a period, or they from us.

We need these changes occasionally in order to find new relations—this in a twofold sense. By such changes there come to our minds more clearly the better qualities of those with whom we are in constant association; we lose sight of the little frictions and irritations that arise; we see how we can be more considerate, appreciative, kind.

In one of those valuable essays of Prentice Mulford entitled "Who Are Our Relations?" he points us to the fact, and with so much insight and common sense, that our relations are not always or necessarily those related to us by blood ties, those of our immediate households, but those most nearly allied to us in mind and in spirit, many times those we have never seen, but that we shall sometime, somewhere be drawn to through the ceaselessly working Law of Attraction, whose basis is that like attracts like. And so in staying too closely with the accustomed relations we may miss the knowledge and the companionship of those equally or even more closely related.

We need these changes to get the kinks out of our minds, our nerves, our muscles—the cobwebs off our faces. We need them to whet again the edge of appetite. We need them to invite the mind and the soul to new possibilities and powers. We need them in order to come back with new implements, or with implements redressed, sharpened, for the daily duties. It is like the chopper working too long with axe unground. There comes the time when an hour at the stone will give it such persuasive power that he can chop and cord in the day what he otherwise would in two or more, and with far greater ease and satisfaction.

We need periods of being by ourselves — alone. Sometimes a fortnight or even a week will do wonders for one, unless he or she has drawn too heavily upon the account. The simple custom, moreover, of taking an hour, or even a half hour, alone in the quiet, in the midst of the daily routine of life, would be the source of inestimable gain for countless numbers.

If such changes can be in closer contact with the fields and with the flowers that are in them, the stars and the sea that lies open beneath them, the woods and the wild things that are of them, one cannot help but find himself growing in love for and an ever fuller appreciation of these, and being at the same time so remade and unfolded that his love, his care, and his consideration for all mankind and for every living creature, will be the greater.

5. To do our own thinking, listening quietly to the opinions of others, but to be sufficiently men and women to act always upon our own convictions.

Sincerity and honesty in thought is a characteristic essential to a commanding, to say nothing of a self-respecting, manhood or womanhood. It distinguishes always the man and the woman of influence.

Essentially true are the words of Robert Louis Stevenson: "If you teach a man to keep his eyes upon what others think of him, unthinkingly to lead the life and hold the principles of the majority of his contemporaries, you must discredit in his eyes the authoritative voice of his own soul. He may be a docile citizen; he will never be a man. It is ours, on the other hand, to disregard this babble and chattering of other men better and worse than we are, and to walk straight before us by what light we have. They may be right; but so, before heaven, are we. They may know; but we know also, and by that knowledge we must stand or fall. There is such a thing as loyalty to a man's own better self; and from those who have not that, God help me, how am I to look for loyalty to others?" To live not as slaves to, nor as unthinking or blind followers of the thought of others, under the mental domination of no man or woman or organization, in family life, in religious life, in community life, on the one hand, and to be not bigoted nor to pose as eccentric in thought and consequent act on the other, to yield and to use good sense in yielding quickly and quietly in non-essentials where peace and harmony will be preserved and where injury will be done no one thereby, is the part of the wise.

True and abundantly suggestive is the thought of Edward Carpenter: "Him who is not detained by mortal adhesions, who walks in the world, yet not of it — Taking part in everything with equal mind, with free limbs and senses unentangled — Giving all, accepting all, using all, enjoying all, asking nothing, shocked at nothing— Him all creatures worship — all men and women bless."

Equally true on the other hand are the words of Joubert: "Those who never retract their opinions love themselves more than they love truth."

Any organization, religious or whatever its nature, that seeks to take from its followers or keep its adherents from perfect freedom and independence — in other words, common honesty — in thought and life does them untold injury, as well as sows thereby the seeds of its own destruction and disintegration. If old and decrepit, fast losing ground and making frantic efforts to hold its adherents, it indicates that the law is finally at work compelling restitution of that which it has filched, the disintegration of that which was untruthfully and unholily built.

If young and even though still apparently growing and rapidly increasing, it is merely a matter of time when violated law will strike its account and its at-one-time most enthusiastic followers will say, "Away with it all! Its falsity and its injury outweighs its good; that which robs me of my man-hood henceforth is not for me!"

Far better to build more truthfully even though it means a little more slowly - it pays in the end. Only those things that are essentially true at their foundations are the permanent.

6. To do our duty as we see it, regardless of the opinion of others - seeming gain or loss, temporary blame or praise.

Independence in the performance of one's duty as he sees it, in living his life as it comes to him to live it, is the natural concomitant of sincerity and independence in thought. To live one's life as it comes to him, to live it in essentials, considerate always of the feelings, the beliefs, the customs, the welfare of others in non-essentials, brings a completeness and a balance to life that makes for contentment as well as for growth and continual attainment.

Handing one's individuality over to the beliefs of the whims or the customs of others is productive of good to no one. Kingly and never too oft-repeated are the words of intrepid Walt Whitman:

"From this hour I ordain myself loos'd of limits and imaginary lines, Going where I list, my own master total and absolute, Listening to others, considering well what they say, Pausing, searching, receiving, contemplating, Gently, but with undeniable will divesting Myself of the holds that would hold me."

Essentially the same truth had Channing in mind when he said: "In proportion as a man suppresses his conviction to save his orthodoxy from suspicion, or distorts language from its common use that he may stand well with his party, in that proportion he clouds and degrades his intellect, as well as undermines the integrity of his character." The blind following of party simply because one chances to belong to a particular party, and many times because his father or uncle — in some tomorrow his mother or his aunt — belonged to it, has been one of the chief causes of the most notorious political corruption and debauchery. It is due to this fact more than to anything else that bosses and machines have been able to get and to retain the hold they have gotten, and in the name of party fealty have been able to thieve the rights and the natural possessions of the people for their own aggrandizement and enrichment. It is only when you and I and all average men fully comprehend the moral obligation that is contained in the phrase, "Independence in party action," that we will see the power of corruption that they now hold slipping from their hands. It is when we not only make it known by quick and decisive action that we will support our own party when its platform is essentially the best and when it is constructed for the purpose of being fulfilled and not for the pure purpose of deception, in whole or in part, and again when its candidates are the best men that can be named; but that we will as quickly support the opposing party when platform and candidates in it are the better, that we will give birth to a revolution of tremendous import in our political and social traditions and life.

Then when we are able to get away from the idea that government is something separate and apart from us, but that in a very fundamental sense we are government so to speak, and when we set about doing for ourselves that which we now hand over to others to be done for us, and many times fully and treacherously done, we will have political institutions of which we and all men will be justly and unreservedly proud.

7. To remain in nature always sweet and simple and humble, and therefore strong.

Sweetness of nature, simplicity in manners and conduct, humility without self-abasement, give the truly kingly quality to men, the queenly to women, the winning to children, whatever the rank or the station may be. The life dominated by this characteristic, or rather these closely allied characteristics, is a natural wellspring of joy to itself and sheds a continual benediction upon all who come within the scope of its influence. It makes for a life of great beauty in itself, and it imparts courage and hope and buoyancy to all others.

If the life find its lot in the more common, the more lowly walks, then for one to go about the daily work and duties doing all things well and with cheerful mind and heart, happy in the present and with full faith as to the working out of all things well and as is for the greatest good in the future, such a life is one of most royal success.

And oh the vast numbers of such kingly and queenly lives in our so-called common walks — men and women doing their daily work, rearing their children, meeting their problems, even their losses or apparent losses, with smiles on their lips and faith and therefore courage in their hearts, turning what would otherwise be drudgery and heartless and unremitting toil into triumphant living. It is this great army that constitutes the very backbone of our nation — of any nation. The very contemplation of this multitude is in itself an inspiration; and it recalls us to a renewed and more steadfast faith in our common human nature.

On the other hand there is no quality that constitutes a more accurate earmark of real greatness and nobility of character in the case of the prosperous and successful, the better known, than the preservation of due humility and simplicity; the life of every man truly great is permeated always with these qualities. An undue sense of one's importance or of one's achievements or possessions, or an undue propensity for show or desire for recognition, indicates always a weak mental strain that may make an otherwise successful and honorable life a failure.

And why should there be anything but simplicity on the part of even the greatest? There will be due humility in it bye and bye; everything here will come to naught; and after its separation from the body the life will pass on into the next state, taking with it only, by way of desirable possessions, all attainment made through the unfoldment of its higher self, all that it has gained by way of self-mastery and nobility of character — and of these attributes none are more enduring, as well as more to be desired, than kindness and humility.

Truly descriptive of the well-balanced man are these lines of Lowell:
"The wisest man could ask no more of fate than to be simple, modest, manly, true, Safe from the many, honored by the few; Nothing to crave in Church or World or Stale, But inwardly in secret to be great."

The one who has true inward greatness thinks little of and cares less for what we term fame. For truly, "Fame means nothing to those who take an inward view of life, for they see that at best it is but the symbol of intrinsic worth."

8. To play the part of neither fool nor knave by attempting to judge another, but to give that same time to living more worthily ourselves.

HE Who is perfect is in the position, were he so minded, of judging another. No man is perfect; no man therefore stands fully in such position.

The fool or the knave alone will do so. The fool because he hasn't sense sufficiently keen to grasp the inconsistency, the foolhardiness of one, imperfect himself, assuming to judge the life of another likewise imperfect. The knave because although keen enough to realize his own shortcomings, his own imperfect life, he voluntarily assumes the role of the hypocrite in passing judgement upon another.

Only the perfect and the all — wise is in the position to judge the innermost life — the springs of the outer life of his fellowmen. Such, however, would be most deliberate in his conclusions and most lenient in his judgements. Deliberate because of his knowledge of the warrings, the weaknesses, and the at times poor or one-sided equipment in the majority of lives which makes their efforts seem almost god-like, could we see all, even when for the time being the entire battle would seem lost. Deliberate, also, because of his refusal to pass judgement upon a life not yet complete. Lenient in his judgement because of the remembrance of his own weaknesses and struggles and failures — better known to himself than to any others — that he passed through in attaining his present perfect state.

It is so easy to see and to point to the fallings of another; it is so difficult to be in the position where there is absolute perfection in ourselves. It is so easy in conversation, idly, jokingly, or with little motives or malices that lie hidden at least in our own minds — and we are sufficiently ostrich-like many times to think in the minds of others — to dwell upon the peculiarities, the shortcomings of the one or ones under consideration. If with a sense always of one's own peculiarities and shortcomings, then it may be partly excusable or at least endurable, but without this it is a humorous manifestation of either ignorant or knavish conceit; and when it comes to the gossip he or she is generally a liar, consciously or unconsciously.

The grander natures and the more thoughtful are always looking for and in conversation dwelling on the better things in others. It is the rule with but few, if any exceptions, that the more noble and worthy and thoughtful the nature, the more it is continually looking for the best there is to be found in every life. Instead of judging or condemning, or acquiring the habit that eventually leads to this, it is looking more closely to and giving its time to living more worthily itself.

It is in this way continually unfolding and expanding in beauty and in power; it is finding an ever-increasing happiness by the admiration and the love that such a life is always, even though all unconsciously, calling to itself from all sources. It is the life that pays by many fold.

9. To get up immediately when we stumble, face again to the light, and travel on without wasting even a moment in regret.

WE are on the way from the imperfect to the perfect; someday, in this life or in some other, we shall reach our destiny. It is as much the part of folly to waste time and cripple our forces in vain, unproductive regrets in regard to the occurrences of the past as it is to cripple our forces through fears and forebodings for the future.

There is no experience in any life which if rightly regarded, rightly turned and thereby wisely used, cannot be made of value; many times things thus turned and used can be made sources of inestimable gain; ofttimes they become veritable blessings in disguise.

All have stumbled — all do stumble. All have fallen; every one of us has fallen flat, at some time, in one way or another, each along the lines of his own peculiar mental or physical makeup. Many a man, many a woman, has had a good round half dozen years or even more clipped from his or her life in moping, in vain and absolutely foolish regrets for this or that occurrence or series of occurrences in the past, thereby blocking initiative and neutralizing powers that rightly used would have led speedily to actualizing the attainment of the conditions desired.

Happy, happy and thrice blessed are we when we are wise enough to learn this quickly, and when we stumble, when we stumble and fall — yes flat — to give sufficient time in looking over the ground in quick attention to the object or the circumstances that caused it, and then with renewed effort getting ourselves together again and going straight on without losing another moment of time in vain, in costly get-no-where regrets. We should be as lenient in judgement of ourselves as we are of others, remembering that all in all we are no better and no worse than the majority of men. We should give ourselves no mental and thereby physical handicaps that will hinder or possibly prevent us in attaining the best that the fullest life holds for us.

Of special value to the one prone to waste time and to turn much of life's joy into bitterness is the thought of Emerson:

"Finish every day and be done with it. You have done what you could. Some blunders and absurdities no doubt crept in; forget them as soon as you can. Tomorrow is a new day; begin it well and serenely, and with too high a spirit to be cumbered with your old nonsense. Today is all that is good and fair. It is too dear with its hopes and invitations to waste a moment on the yesterdays." And again: "Our strength grows out of our weakness. The indignation which arms itself with secret forces does not awaken until we are pricked and stung and sorely assailed. A great man is always willing to be little. Whilst he sits on the cushion of advantages he goes to sleep. When he is pushed, tormented, defeated, he has a chance to learn something; he has been put on his wits, on his manhood; he has gained facts, learns his ignorance, is cured of the insanity of conceit, has got moderation and real skill."

10. To love and to hold due reverence for all people and all things, but to stand in awe or fear of nothing save our own wrong-doing.

GOD never made any man or any institution a dispenser of truth or the custodian of the mental life of another. He instituted laws and forces whereby one man by ordering his life in accordance with the highest laws and forces of his being, living so to speak in the upper stories of his being, has become the revealer of truth and the exampler of truth to other men.

In the degree, however, that he has been worthy of receiving and successful in living, and thus in transmitting such revelations, in that degree has he kept his own personality in the background in order that the truth might be free from encumbrances now and from encrustations bye and bye. In other words, in the degree that he has loved truth more and self or self-aggrandizement less has he lost sight of himself in order that the truth might be unencumbered and freely and effectively delivered.

To hold undue reverence for or to stand in awe or fear of another is an exhibition, though perchance unconscious, of a lack of faith in or a degradation of our own native powers and forces, which if rightly unfolded and used might open to us revelations and lead us to heights even beyond those of the one we mentally crouch before.

There is probably no mental habit, native or acquired, that brings us so much that is undesirable in life as fear. It has been, it is today, the one great bugbear in almost countless lives, and until we redeem ourselves from this filcher of the best in life, we stand in fear at one time or another of almost everything. There is fear when happy that happiness will not remain; fear — when miserable that this condition will always remain; fear for our friends in that we shall lose them; fear of our enemies, if sufficiently unwise as to have them, in that they are continually at work in harm to us or to our reputations in the minds of others; fear of poverty in that what is ours today will not be ours tomorrow; fear of the elements; fear of sickness; fear of the transition we call death, either in our own case or in the case of those near to us. We fear that the bogy man, whatever his form and equipment and purpose, is continually on the wake for us. And so our conversation runs in terms of fear, and the prevailing mental attitude of fear has become the fixed habit of countless thousands.

It moreover stamps itself and registers its baneful influences in the very bodies of its victims. Fear retards and even paralyzes healthy action, the same as worry — closely allied to it — stagnates, corrodes, and pulls it down. When, moreover, we once understand the subtle power of thought — thought as a force — and its law in that like builds like and like attracts like, we can see how we endow the very things we fear with power to get their hold and work their ills upon us. Thus we create within us and we attract to us, many times all unconsciously, conditions the very opposite of those we would have in our lives.

Fear is, so to speak, the direct opposite of faith, and faith is perhaps the strongest and most effective mental-spiritual force that we can possess or grow. To take the positive, the cheerful attitude of mind, bidding good-bye to fear and setting about resolutely for the actualization of those conditions that are good and desirable, we thus set into operation silent but subtle and all-powerful forces that will work for us continual good. In this way fear will gradually lose its hold and we will find ourselves becoming masters instead of, as formerly, creatures of circumstance.

11. To recognize the good lying at the heart of all people, of all things, waiting for expression, all in its own good way and time.

WE are in a life of growth and unfoldment, in a world of change and incompleteness; each thing is good in its place, and each thing has its own particular and peculiar purpose. Each life is divine at its center and some time will show forth in the full beauty of holiness, which is wholeness or completeness — divine self-realization.

Aptness or tardiness in recognizing the source and also the laws of our being, combined with varied innate tendencies to start with or combined with the influences of varied environments, is ordinarily the reason why one life differs from another at any given period in its moral, ethical tone or fibre. Quickness also or tardiness in coming into a conscious living realization of the essential oneness of each life and all life with the divine, the source, the center, the substance of all life that there is manifested in existence, and the avenues of wisdom and of power that such realization opens, determines the relative condition of any life at any given time.

Sometimes, frequently, a year in the life thus awake to its real nature gives by way of insight, growth, unfoldment, therefore of peace, of happiness, of usefulness, more than a previous fifty years rolled. together, and when it comes to a life that we are inclined to belittle, to judge harshly, to throw stones at, it behooves us to be guarded as the wise are guarded, for when the awakening and the consequent rapid march of such a soul begins it may quickly pass beyond those that we today deem much higher and much more important, beyond ourselves.

In a certain sense, in the broad sense, all is good. Yes, apparent misfortune and even what we ordinarily term evil, in that it is the good in the making. If we have faith, if we have patience and perseverance, there is no condition, no experience that rightly viewed and rightly turned and used will not bring us stores of good.

Everything that comes into each life has its place and its purpose, its part to play, and were it not necessary or were it not good in the long run that it come it would not come. If there is a divine order in the universe, if there is law — and in a sense there is absolutely nothing but law — it cannot be otherwise. A clear comprehension of this fact, or if this be impossible, a mere belief in it, is of tremendous value in helping us to meet understandingly and to work intelligently and bravely in the midst of adverse or undesirable conditions, that we may push on and through them to those that are more valuable and desirable. It is of value by way of enabling us to adjust ourselves in friendly relations with our environment or with existing conditions as long as it is well or possibly essential that we remain there, and to look for and to get the good that is unquestionably there for us.

By living thus in harmony, if not always in fullest sympathy with such conditions, we adopt the best possible method of getting from them the greatest good, and pushing on through them, not only with the least possible handicap, but with added wisdom and power. And possibly to some to whom the way may seem already long, this thought from Browning may be of value:

"The common problem, yours, mine, everyone's, is not to fancy what were fair in life provided it could be — but finding first what may be, then find how to make it fair up to our means: a very different thing."

12. To know that it is the middle ground that brings pleasure and satisfaction, and that excesses have to be paid for ofttimes with heavy and sometimes with frightful costs.

ALL things, good in themselves, are for use and enjoyment; but all things must be rightly used in order that there may be full and lasting enjoyment. A law written into the very fibre of human life, so to speak, is to the effect that excesses, the abuse of anything good in itself, will end disastrously, so that one's pleasures and enjoyments will have to be gathered up for repairs, or perchance his shattered mind or body also, and in case of the latter then the former will have to bide their time or wait indefinitely for their resumption.

Wise indeed is he who fully recognizes this law that never has and that never will allow itself to be violated or undone, but that will shatter, sometimes with telling and open blows, more often perhaps with blows subtle and guarded, but just as telling, the happiness or even the mind and the body of the one who would do violence to or who would fail to recognize its mandate — Moderation.

On the other hand, to see evil in things good in themselves is the perversion of another law that carries with it its own peculiar penalty. The one tends to make the prig, the self-righteous, out of a good, wholesome man or woman, the same as the other makes eventually the voluptuary. The one errs in the one direction the same as the other in another direction. Each pays the penalty for his folly, the one by cutting himself off from much innocent and valuable God intended enjoyment, at the same time casting a continual shadow over the lives of others; the other by way of settling heavy bills of costs for his excesses.

It should be then neither license nor perverted use on the one hand, nor asceticism or priggishness on the other — the full use of all normal and natural functions, faculties, and powers, innocent and good in themselves, that all may be brought to their fullest growth and development, but never excessive or perverted use.

The tendency of the great majority, especially in our present day American life, is on the side of the too serious, the too busy, the too absorbing in the business, in the work. This induces all unconsciously, in time, a prevailing type of thought and mental activity that takes, so to speak, the buoyancy, the elasticity out of both mind and body, so that age and its accompanying features manifest, assert, and fix themselves in many, or to speak more truly, in the majority of cases, long before their time. By way of balance, by way of disarming these, we need more of the play element, more of the open air, the sunshine, the exercise element in our lives. It would save thousands from stiffening of joints and muscles, hardened arteries, dyspepsia, apoplexy, nerve exhaustion, melancholia, premature age, premature death.

"Happy recreation has a very subtle influence upon one's ability, which is emphasized and heightened and multiplied by it. How our courage is braced up, our determination, our ambition, our whole outlook on life changed by it! There seems to be a subtle fluid from humor and fun which penetrates the entire being, bathes all the mental faculties, and washes out the brain-ash and debris from exhausted cerebrum and muscles. . . . A joyful, happy, fun-loving environment develops powers, resources, and possibilities which would remain latent in a cold, dull, repressing atmosphere."

Look where we will, in or out and around us, we will find that it is the middle ground — neither poverty nor excessive riches, good wholesome use without license, a turning into the bye-ways along the main road where innocent and healthy God-sent and God-intended pleasures and enjoyments are to be found; but never getting far enough away to lose sight of the road itself. The middle ground it is that the wise man or woman plants foot upon.

13. To know that work, occupation, something definite and useful to do, is one of the established conditions of happiness in life.

IT is difficult to know, much more to tell, why there is such a law; but perchance it is that work, definite, useful activity, and along with it the satisfaction of accomplishment, is necessary to growth and development, and unquestionably growth, development, attainment is the purpose, the object of life. However this may be, we know one thing, that we always feel better when we can look back when night comes and feel that the day has been good in accomplishment, or at least in effort, and that it has not been allowed to pass without some good, some useful thing accomplished, to its credit.

Are we alone in the thought that work is one of the established conditions of successful and therefore healthy, happy living? Of its purpose, or rather its place, Hugh Black has given utterance to this thought: "One thing is certain, that, though work itself will not insure happiness, yet without it happiness is impossible. It is an essential condition of a contented life. This has been the experience of all, and there is no more useful lesson for youth to learn early." It was Amiel who said: "It is work that gives flavor to life. Mere existence without object and without effort is a poor thing. Idleness leads to languor, and languor to disgust." Zola, putting it a little too strongly perhaps, showing nevertheless his thought regarding it, says: "Work! It is the sole law of the world "; and again: "Let each one accept his task, a task which should fill his life. It may be very humble; it will not be the less useful. Never mind what it is, so long as it exists and keeps you erect. When you have regulated it without excess — just the quantity you are able to accomplish each day — it will cause you to live in health and in joy."

Putting his general thought along the same line in more poetic form, Barry Cornwall wrote:
"There is not a creature from England's king
To the peasant that delves the soil,
That knows half the pleasures the seasons bring,
If he have not his share of toil."
A still more inclusive truth Bayard Taylor has put in the verse;
"Sloth is sin and toil is worship, and the soul demands an aim;
Who neglects the ordination, he shall not escape the blame."

But here again it is the middle ground — neither idleness nor excessive toil. Work, whatever its nature — so-called great or menial, cabinet minister or street cleaner, celebrated singer or homekeeper or shirt stitcher — work that is glorified and made a fair contributor to a genuinely religious life by the spirit we carry into it, by the way we do it. It is this and this alone that determines whether it is really great or menial — work, earnest and sincere, that is broken by periods of rest and leisure, so that the latter become replete with enjoyment and value. This combining of work with rest and play, of rest and play with work, gives zest and spirit to both and brings again in this phase of our being the balance to life.

God, however, deliver us from the too earnest people, those whose work is so important that they can never find place for the time off, whose earnestness leads to inflation, or to a stealing of responsibility for many important — or less important — things from God, who have no time for the appreciation or the development of a sense of humour and the occasional levity, who eliminate the innocent pleasures and leisures and joys that a good, sensible, well-rounded and withal useful life takes as its portion. By being too valuable to our fellowmen we may often become of but little value to them, and eventually to ourselves; here again, therefore, it is the middle ground.

The chief use, perhaps, of passing through the period of self-importance, of excessive earnestness, especially if it be in comparative youth, is that then we are through with it, we are able in reflection to get an occasional enjoyment by being able to see the humour of it all, and we are able also to appreciate it quickly and to see the humour of it in the occasional other one who is still in its throes.

For the all round life there must be the balance also as to the kinds of work. The hand, manual, ground worker, to insure the most happy and satisfying life for himself, to say nothing of his greater value to his community, to the state, must turn periodically into the intellectual bye-ways, through investigation, study, reading, a greater intelligence of the best and latest developments and findings in his own work, as well as keeping in touch with general progress. This will determine whether he remain or become a mere machine or an intelligent, commanding worker, as also a valuable citizen.

The brain worker, the business man, and especially the one doing creative mental work, if he would know the all-round joy of living, must have that to turn to whereby his hands, his body, get their normal, healthy activity, and if it be useful, constructive work, or work in or of the soil, the greater the interest and value. This would save almost countless thousands of good men and good women that overwrought, nervous, brain and nerve fagged condition that renders full enjoyment of anything impossible, that causes a craving for and a turning to stimulants, excitement, extravagances that only increase their difficulties. It would save them to the simple, healthy, homely, and lasting joys that nature rewards never with satiety, but with good sleep, good appetite, good digestion, in brief, that greatest of all earthly blessings — good health.

14. To realize always clearly that thoughts are forces, that like creates like and like attracts like, and that to determine one's thinking, therefore, is to determine his life.

THAT we have within us the force or the power that makes us what we are, and that we have it in our own hands to determine how that force, that power, shall be used is a revelation, if not clearly realized before, of tremendous import to any life.

One of the most valuable, not discoveries, but rather rediscoveries, of the present decade, or still better, perhaps, clear formulations of a long-known truth, is the fact that thoughts are forces, that they have form and quality and substance and power, that they are the silent, unseen, but subtle agents at work that are daily and hourly producing and determining, and with almost absolute precision, the conditions in our lives. As is the inner, therefore, so always and necessarily is the outer. What one lives in his thought world is continually forming and thus determining his outer material world.

The clearly established law of thought as a force is that like creates like and like attracts like. The hopeful, cheerful, confident find themselves continually growing in faith, in confident, healthy optimism, in courage; they are also continually attracting and drawing to themselves, thus gaining as friends and helpers those of similar qualities and possessions, and they are likewise inspiring these qualities in others. Courage and faith beget energy and power; energy and power rightly directed bring success. Such, as a rule, are the successful people — successful simply by way of natural law.

The fearing, grumbling, worrying, vascillating do not succeed in anything and generally live by burdening, in some form or another, someone else. They stand in the way of, they prevent their own success; they fail in living even an ordinary healthy, normal life; they cast a blighting influence over and they act as a hindrance to all with whom they at any time come in contact. The pleasures we take captive in life, the growth and advancement we make, the pleasure and benefit our company or acquaintanceship brings to others, the very desirability of our companionship on the part of others — all depend upon the types of thought we entertain and live most habitually with.

Not only is there the direct connection — that of cause and effect — between the types of thought we most habitually entertain and the value and joy of living in our own lives, as well as the pleasure we give and the influence we exert upon others, but the intimate relations existing between certain mental states and the various bodily functions are beginning now to be so clearly understood and can be so easily traced and established, that no clear thinking, open mind can fail to recognize the great power constantly at work for disease or for health; and if certain given mental states or habits induce diseased conditions and structure, as they do, then certain other mental states, especially when consciously and definitely directed, can antidote and remove obstructions so that the operation of the life forces within can undo and cure the same.

There is a general order of thought that may be described as the normal, health bringing, pleasure bringing, the desirable, valuable. Of this order are faith, hope, love, magnanimity, charity, nobility of feeling and purpose, good temper, goodwill, clear, clean, hopeful, healthful thought. These are evidently the God-intended, for they are productive of wholesome activity, of health and strength and peace of mind, of soul, and of body.

There is a general order of thought that may be described as abnormal, perverted, and carrying with it a slow, corroding, poisoning effect upon or a quick death-sting for all that is good, healthy, and desirable in life. Of this order are fear, worry, anxiety, resentment, envy, jealousy, hatred, revenge, ill-temper, nagging, fault-finding, lust. The effect of this order of thought if lived in to any extent is that of a retarding, corroding, poisoning effect upon mind, soul, and through them the body — upon the latter not by way of fanciful influence, but by way of direct chemical corroding and poisoning, with its resultant effect upon tissues and structure. Thus one in time becomes the victim of the products, the children of his own brain-his thoughts.

Says one of our modern keen thinkers and forceful writers: "We are beginning to see that we can renew our bodies by renewing our thoughts; change our bodies by changing our thoughts; that by holding the thought of what we wish to become, we can become what we desire. Instead of being the victims of fate we can order our fate, we can largely determine what it shall be. Our destiny changes with our thought. We shall become what we wish to become when our habitual thought corresponds with the desire.... He is a fortunate man who early learns the secret of scientific brain-building, and who acquires the inestimable art of holding the right suggestion in his mind, so that he can triumph over the dominant note in his environment when it is unfriendly to his highest good.... The whole body is really a projected mind, objectified, made tangible. It is an outpicturing of the mind in material form. When we look at a person we actually see the mind, or what his thinking has made him.... The life follows the thought. There is no law clearer than that. There is no getting away from it." (*Dr. O. S. Marden in Success Magazine, August, 1908.)

After a certain age is reached in any life, the prevailing tone and condition of that life is the resultant of the mental habits of that life. If one has mental equipment sufficient to find and to make use of the Science of Thought in its application to scientific mind and body building, habit and character building, there is little by way of heredity, environment, attainment of which he or she will not be the master.

One thing is very certain — the mental points of view, the mental tendencies and habits at twenty eight and thirty eight will have externalized themselves and will have stamped the prevailing conditions of any life at forty eight and fifty eight and sixty eight.

15. To take and to live always in the attitude of mind that compels gladness, looking for and thus drawing to us continually the best in all people and all things, being thereby the creators of our own good fortunes.

Cheerfulness, looking on the bright side of things, seeing the humorous side of situations when others see only the "too-bad," the "provoking," the "spasm," the "isn't-it-terrible," is a matter of habit quite as much as it is a matter of aptitude. If one lack the habit he fails in one of the most important or even essential qualities of his life; so, on the other hand, to cultivate it to its highest is to become possessor of a quality in life most eagerly to be sought.

The optimistic, cheerful, hopeful habit of mind and thought is continually putting into and keeping in operation silent subtle forces that are continually changing from the unseen into the seen, from the ideal into the actual, and attracting to us, from without, conditions of a nature kindred to the type of thought force that we give birth to and set into operation. Ordinarily we find in people those qualities we are mostly looking for; if we show to them our best, their best will open and show itself to us.

There is no quality that exerts more good, is of greater service to all mankind during the course of the ordinary life, than the mind and the heart that goes out in an all embracing love for all, that is the generator and the circulator of a genuine, hearty, wholesome sympathy and courage and good cheer, that is not disturbed or upset by the passing occurrence little or great, but that is serene, tranquil, and conquering to the end, that is looking for the best, that is finding the best, and that is inspiring the best in all. There is, moreover, no quality that when genuine brings such rich returns to its possessor by virtue of the thoughts and the feelings that it inspires and calls forth from others and that come back laden with their peaceful, stimulating, healthful influences for him.

On the other hand, the peevish, gloomy, grumbling, paniky, critical — the small — cast a sort of deadening, unwholesome influence wherever they go. They get, however, what they give, for they inspire and call back to themselves thoughts and feelings of the kind they are sufficiently stupid to allow a dominating influence in their own lives. People ruled by the mood of gloom attract to themselves gloomy people and gloomy conditions, those that are of no help to them, but rather a hindrance.

The cheerful, confident, tranquil in all circumstances are continually growing in these same qualities, for the mind grows by and in the direction of that which it feeds upon. This process of mental chemistry is continually working in our lives, bringing us desirable or undesirable conditions according to our prevailing mental states.

The course of determining resolutely to expect only those things which we desire, or which will be ultimately for our larger good, of thinking health and strength rather than disease and weakness, an abundance for all our needs rather than poverty, success rather than failure, of looking for and calling from others the best there is in them, is one of the greatest aids also to bodily health and perfection. As a rule one seldom knows of those of this trend or determination of mind complaining of physical ailments, because they are generally free from the long list of ailments and disabilities that have their origin in perverted emotional and mental states, that by being regularly fed are allowed to externalize themselves and become settled conditions.

This attitude of mind is the one also that carries us through when the dark day comes and things look their worst. It enables us to take the long view, to throw the thought on beyond the present day, difficulty, or depression to the time when it will have worked itself out all well and good. Such times come to all. We must be brave and bravely take our share.

It is how we bear ourselves at such times that determines our real worth and use, whether we have stamina, backbone, courage — real character — and if at such times we can stand unfaltering, uncomplaining, desirous of neither sympathy nor pity, patient but resolute, and doing today what today reveals to be done and so ready for the morrow when it comes, there can be but one outcome. The Higher Powers of all the universe stand back of such a life, they uphold it, they sustain it, they stamp it with success, they crown it with adoration and with honour.

<Back

16. To know that the ever conscious realization of the essential oneness of each life with the Divine Life is the highest of all knowledge, and that to open ourselves as opportune channels for the Divine Power to work in and through us is the open door to the highest attainment, and to the best there is in life.

FOR a life of the larger growth and attainment, for a life that finds itself ready for whatever the emergency that confronts it along the way, it is essential that it find a basis, or as has been aptly said, its center. It must be, moreover, a basis, a center that its own intelligence, its own thought can find and give acceptance to, not something imposed from without by some other mind, or body of men, or institution.

To me there is nothing more rational, more reasonable than to find one's start in being — that Spirit of Infinite Life and Power that is the intelligence, the unfolder, the creator if you please, of all there is in this universe of evident design of law and order. It is a universe where there is, in a sense, nothing but law, law constantly working through the agency of cause and effect, and in which for even the most ordinary intelligence to think that there is only, or that there is the slightest element of chance, is practically incomprehensible.

If all is in absolute accordance with law and plan and order, there is an intelligence, a power that is back of and that gives life and form and sustaining force to that law and order. To me this is being manifesting itself in existence, the Supreme Intelligence — God. The Creator manifesting itself — himself if you prefer — in creation, so that Creator and creation are one, in the sense that Creator is the life, the spirit of all there is in existence — in creation. There is the one life, this Spirit of Infinite Life and Power that is back of all, working in and through all, the Life of all. To speak therefore of our life as separate and apart from this Infinite Life, as separate from the life of God, is impossible. To speak of it as equal to the life of God is unreasonable. In nature, in essence, in quality it is essentially one and the same, therefore Divine in its origin, in its essence. In degree of manifestation and in power it is totally different, and here is the one essential feature of this all important fact in its bearing upon our lives. It is possible for us to remain closed to, in ignorance of, the source and nature of our real being, and to live without a conscious connection with this Source.

It is the mind that relates the soul of man, the real eternal self, with this Source. It is through the instrumentality of the mind that we are enabled to make this conscious connection. It is this that distinguishes us from the inanimate world; our minds, moreover, are given us for use.

It is possible for us through the channel of our minds so to relate ourselves to, and to grow ever more conscious of, the real identity of our lives with their Divine Source that we become receivers and liberators, so to speak, of the attributes of the Divine Life. Among the attributes of this Life are wisdom, power, love, harmony. In the degree that we make and keep this conscious connection we make ourselves natural channels for a continually greater degree of Divine Intelligence and Power to manifest in and through us.

It is in a way like the plant. When in its right relations with that to which it must rightly relate itself for unfoldment and growth — soil with sufficient moisture and sunlight — its life and growth go on naturally and unimpeded, and it finally reaches its destiny — fullness of unfoldment and growth, which means maturity. If but poorly related to or if separated from these, it struggles for a while and finally withers and dies.

Let us recur to the statement: In the degree that we make and keep this conscious connection with our Source do we make ourselves natural channels for a continually greater degree of Divine Intelligence and Power to manifest in and through us. And what, it is but right to ask, is the basis of such a statement outside of the statement itself? The fact that it is the uniform experience of all who become awake to this New Consciousness, as multitudes are becoming awake to it today. It has likewise been the experience of thousands in the world's history, both men and women, whose names and works are familiar to all, of the mystical, of the truly religious — not necessarily institutional and generally not — trend of mind and purpose of life. The religious mind and life, because the fundamental principle, in brief the essence of all real religion, whatever its form or time or name, is: The consciousness of God in the soul of man. It is the full realization, "In Him we live and move and have our being." It is the Christ state that Jesus realized and lived continually in because of the complete realization of the oneness of his life with the Father's life. "I and the Father are one." "The words that I speak unto you I speak not of myself, but the Father that dwelleth in me, He doeth the works " — and it is thus that he becomes the Saviour of other men, by virtue of pointing out to them this same way.

This brings also the child simplicity, for in ourselves we are nothing; we have every conceivable type of limitation. In the degree that the God life with its attendant wisdom and power dwells in us through our opening the way, in that degree do our latent possibilities change to actualized power. In other words, we determine our own limitations. In the degree that we come into the knowledge of our real selves our limitations rise and we come thereby into actual possession of our own.

And what, it is only right again to ask, has this to do with the healthy, bountiful, practical, everyday life that is the real thing before us? This consciousness of the God life in the soul, so that it becomes the constant guiding force in our lives, is nothing more nor less than the finding of the Kingdom. It is testing the reality of the injunction of Jesus, he who knew whereof he spoke when he said, "Seek ye first the Kingdom of God and His righteousness, and all these things shall be added unto you." It is the inclusive thing which brings all things of detail in its train.

It brings insight, intuition, wisdom, for it is the very source of wisdom. It brings power, for the secret of all power is the right co-ordination of the agents of expression with the power that works from within. It brings influence, for all men feel instinctively and are influenced, even unconsciously, by such a life.

It is productive of bodily health and vigour, for spirit, from its very nature, can admit of no disease or inharmony, and it externalizes, in the body of him who realizes himself a spiritual being, health and harmony. If inharmony and disease have, gotten their hold before, they are quickly or more gradually eliminated according to the degree of this realization by the reversal of the process whereby they came. It brings power as an agent in healing the bodily ills of another because the mind spiritually alive is able more readily to reach and impress the subconscious mind of another, the agency through which all mental or spiritual healing in oneself or in another is accomplished. In the degree of the completeness of this realization is the element of time in such cases eliminated, as was so abundantly true in Jesus' case, whose (to us) wonderful works of healing were all in accordance with law — and this same law that we are considering.

It brings material things in full abundance, for wisdom offers the key and power unlocks the door; all material things are in the universe now waiting simply for the right combination, the right type of demand, to draw them to their rightful owners. It saves one, moreover, from the excessive accumulation of material things, for the life thus awake realizes that they are not and never, except to our detriment, can be made an end in themselves, but are simply a means to an end.

It eliminates fear, forebodings, worry, for these can have no existence in such a life. It gives a calmness, a poise, a serenity to life that proclaims the man or the woman master of the greatest of all arts — the Art of Living. Such a life has no fear and scarcely a thought of death, for it realizes that the only death to be feared, or that has in any sense a reality, is that feeling or that sense of separateness from the life of God. It has full consciousness of the fact that it is living the eternal life now, that it can never be in that life more in reality than now, and that in all eternity it can never be more conscious of God's presence than is in its power at this very moment. It acknowledges the reality of Jesus wonderful insight when he said: "Say not lo here nor lo there, know ye not that the Kingdom of Heaven is within you?" It is conscious of the fact that it is surrounded, guided, upheld by a force that is not to be explained, perhaps, as to the mode of its working. "No weapon that is formed against thee shall prosper." As real to it as the air it breathes is the ever-conscious fact, "Thou wilt keep him in perfect peace whose mind is stayed on Thee."

The Greatest Thing Ever Known

The greatest thing ever known—What is it? Full surely the answer must be one that is absolutely universal, both in its nature and in the possibilities of its application. It must be one that can be accepted wholly and unreservedly, not only by a single individual, but by bodies of individuals, be they the originators of any particular school of Ethics, the followers of any particular system of Philosophy, or even the adherents of any great system of Religion. It must be one so true in itself that it can be accepted by all men alike the world over. And again, it must be an answer that is true for no particular period of time, but equally true for all time—an answer that was true not only for yesterday, that is true for today, that may be true for tomorrow, but one equally true for yesterday, today, and forever.

In laying our foundation, therefore, it must be laid upon something as true and as certain as Life itself, and as eternal as Everlasting Life. What is as true and as certain as Life itself?—Life, only Life. And what do we mean by this answer? Let us give it for a moment our most careful consideration for upon what we find here depends and rests all that is to follow.

Let us start, then, with that in regard to which all can agree; something taken not from mere tradition, from mere hearsay, but something that comes to us from no source other than our own interior consciousness, our own reason and insight. In other words, let us make our approach, not from the theological standpoint, but from that which is far more certain and satisfactory—the philosophical. Then, and then only, will we allow pure reason to be our guide, and then by having as the earnest desire of both mind and heart, truth, truth for its own sake, and then for the sake of its influence upon everyday life, we will thus allow pure reason to be illumined by the "Light that lighteth every man that cometh into the world."

In the degree that we open ourselves to and are true to this are we on sure and safe ground, for thus are we going directly to the source and the only source of all true revelation. In the degree, on the other hand, that we close ourselves or become untrue to this are we on uncertain and dangerous ground, and liable to find ourselves hopelessly floundering in the quagmire of theological traditions and speculations and doubts, of which the world has already seen so much. Pure reason, therefore, shall be our guide—pure reason illumined by the Inner Light.

Again, then, What is Life? Being is Life. Life is Being. Being, therefore, is our starting-point, and indeed our very foundation itself. Each can form his own idea of being, so that in reality it needs no defining. By it we mean that self-existent Principle of Life and all that attends it, without beginning and without end, the Power, that animates all and so that is the Life of all. In short, we can scarcely define Being, if indeed it can be defined, without using the word Life, and indeed without identifying the two. Being and Life, then, are one and the same. One infinite intelligence expressing Itself as Life.

It is Being that projects itself into existence. Being, acting through its own intelligence, prompted by Love, projected by Will, goes out and takes form. We cannot say that it enters into form, for until it projects itself into existence there is no form, but form comes by virtue of Being, the self-existent Principle of Life and Power, manifesting itself in existence. So in a sense Life, which is one with being, is the soul, and form, of whatever nature the body. Only as Being projects itself into existence are we able to know it. We can know the fact that Being is, but only as it manifests itself in form are we able to know it itself.

Being is one, not many. As Being is the source of all Life, there is, then, only one Life, and this Being is the Life of all. "The One Divine Being, and this alone, is the true Reality in all Existence, and so remains in all Eternity." And there is nothing real that is, or, indeed, that can be, outside of it. True, then, are the words of one of the most highly illumined philosophers of modern times—"Thus we have these two elements: Being, as it is essentially and in itself; and Form, which is assumed by the former in consequence of Existence. But how have we expressed ourselves? What is it that assumes a form? Answer: Being, as it exists in itself without any change whatever in its inward, Essential Nature. But what, then, is there in Existence? Answer: Nothing else than the One Eternal and Unchangeable Being, besides which there can be nothing."

This Being which is Infinite is in truth, then, the Infinite Being, and this Infinite Being is what we mean by God—each using the term that appeals most to himself. Literally, the "I Am," as is signified by the name Jehovah, which is derived in the Hebrew from the words 'To Be.' God, then, is the Infinite Being, the Infinite

Spirit of Life which fills all in existence with Himself alone, so that all is He, since He is All. If God is all, then all must be He, and from this fact there is no escape, and no other conclusion can be arrived at which does not do violence to all rational thought.

There are those—and to such these pages are not addressed, for so limited are they in comprehension, or so closed to Truth and hence so engrossed in bigotry, that they either can or will see nothing that may be opposed to their present ideas—there are those that say that God is all, and immediately begin to fill up the universe with that which God is not. Again, there are those open to and eagerly seeking for the highest Truth who say: "But evil is not God, and how then can God be all, for surely there is such a thing as evil." Certainly evil is not God, nor has God anything to do with evil. Evil is simply the result of the temporary perversion of the good, and as such must either cease or in time die at its own hands, for evil is self-consuming. As such, then, it has no essential reality, for that which has essential reality has neither beginning nor end.

Man is the only one who has to do with evil, he alone is its author; man, who in his thought separates himself from Divine Being in whom alone true happiness and blessedness can be found. Regarding the mere bodily existence as his real life, he tries to find pleasure and happiness entirely through these channels, and many times by violating the higher laws of his being, and thus what we term evil enters in. But though man has perfect freedom in all his thoughts and acts, God will suffer no such violation. And so, from the pain and suffering that result from the violation of the higher laws of his being, he is pushed on in his thought and through this in his life to the Reality of his being, and finds that only in conscious union with God true pleasure and blessedness lie, as God surely intends. True, then, evil is not God, nor has God anything to do with evil, as "God is of too pure eyes to behold evil and cannot look upon iniquity," for man alone has to do with evil, so long, and only so long, as he lives his life outside of a conscious union with the life of God.

Infinite Being, God, then, is the one and the only Life. You and I in our true selves are Life. It cannot be truly said that we have life, for we are Life; Life that manifests itself in the form in existence that we denominate by the term body. And as the Infinite Being, the Infinite Life, God, is the "I Am", the life of all in existence, then we indeed are parts of the Infinite Being, the Infinite Life, the "I Am", of the very God Himself. And thus it is that your life and mine is one with the life of God. By this we do not mean the mere body, but the Real Self that takes to itself the form—body. It is impossible that there be any real life that is not one with the life of God; and in this sense it is true that the life of man and the life of God are essentially and necessarily one and the same. In essence they are one and the same; they differ not in quality, for this is impossible rationally even to conceive of. There is a difference—it is a difference simply in degree, not in essence or kind.

It is only by reason of our own thought that our life is separate from the life of God, only by reason of our own thought that we live in this separation, if indeed we can use the term live where the full life is not consciously realised and enjoyed. Truly, then, "In Him we live and move and have our being." We never could have been and never can be, other than Divine Being. And I fully agree with the thought expressed in a letter from Prof. Max Müller in which he says: "I cannot accept Athanasius when he says that we can become gods; man cannot say, 'become God', because he is God; what else could he be, if God is the only true and real being?" Man is the individualised expression or reflection of God imaged forth and made manifest in bodily form. How is it, then, I hear it asked, that man has the limitations that he has, that he is subject to fears and forebodings, that he is liable to sin and error, that he is the victim of disease and suffering? There is but one reason. He is not living, except in rare cases here and there, in the conscious realisation of his own true Being, and hence of his own true Self.

We must in thought be conscious of who and what we are before the qualities and powers of our real being, and hence our real selves, actualise or even manifest themselves. Says one of the most highly illumined seers of modern times: "The True Life and its Blessedness consists in a union with the Unchangeable and Eternal; but the Eternal can be apprehended only by Thought, and is in no other way approachable by us." Thought is the atmosphere, the element, in a sense the very substance, of the phase of Divine Being that we call human life. How much it is likewise that of other forms of Divine Being in existence, as we see it in the various manifestations of life around us, we cannot be so fully certain of. But certain it is that through thought and through thought alone, we are able to conceive of Divine Being as the Infinite Spirit and Essence of Life, and then to see clearly that it is the Life of our Life, and then to live in the realisation of our oneness with it, and in this way allow the Divine Word to become incarnate in us by being thus fully and completely manifest in us, precisely as it became manifest and hence incarnate in the Christ Jesus, as we shall hereafter find.

When Divine Being manifests itself in physical human form, its inward essential nature or reality changes not, for this from its very nature it is impossible for it in any way to do. It does, however, have to manifest itself through the agency of physical senses, and precisely for this reason is it that for a time our real inward Essential Nature and Life is concealed from us, but this again only by reason of our limited comprehension. When we are born into the world of Nature we see and become aware through and by means of the physical senses, and the natural physical world becomes to us for a time the real world. Eventually, however, through these very senses we are able to conceive of the One and Eternal Source of Life as our real and therefore our only life, and then through them to hold ourselves in this living realisation. Hence, first that which is natural and then that which is spiritual is necessarily as well as literally and philosophically true.

Happy, however, is the man who dwells not long as the purely natural man, but is early transformed into the spiritual, and so in whom the Divine Word early becomes incarnate. Blessed state indeed, says the thoughtful and earnest seeker for the best things in life, and more to be prized than all else besides; but if this state is really possible of realisation, what can be said regarding the method of entering into it? There is only one thing in all the wide universe that will enable you as well as all the world to do it effectually. "Be ye therefore transformed by the renewing of your minds." This is the force, the transforming power, so far as the form of life we denominate by the term human is concerned; this and this alone. True, then, and most welcome is the great fact of facts that the world is beginning to become so conscious of today that "The mind is everything; what you think, you become."

Mortal mind? says one. Yes and no. Strictly speaking, there is no such thing as mortal mind—there is only Divine Mind. When in our own thought, and by reason of our limited comprehension, we shut ourselves off and look upon ourselves as individual physical beings, we give birth to a temporary mode of thought that might well be termed mortal mind, or, rather, the product of mortal mind. But it is at first natural, and it is only by using this "mortal mind" that it is able to be transformed, and hence renewed into the Divine Mind. So by wisely using that which we have, the natural, we are transformed from that which is most apparent, and consequently that which we think we are, the mortal, the physical, into that which from all eternity in reality are, and never except in our minds can get away from,—the Spiritual, the Divine. It is through this instrumentality that the Divine Life within us, the Divine Life with all its ever-ready-to-break-forth glories and powers, is enabled to be changed from a mere passive and hence potential actuality, and to burst forth into the full splendours of conscious, active life.

Surely, then, thought rightly directed and rightly used has within it the true regenerating and hence redeeming power. Through our thought and it alone are we able to make for ourselves a new heaven and a new earth, or, rather, by thus finding the kingdom of God, and through it entering into the conscious realisation of the heavenly state, are we able to make for ourselves a new earth by actualising the kingdom of Heaven in our lives while living on the earth, and which, when once truly realised, can never be lost.

The majority of people are not awake; it is only here and there that we find one even partially awake. Practically all of us, as a result, are living lives that are unworthy almost the name of lives, compared to those we might be living, and that lie within our easy grasp. While it is true that each life is in and of Divine Being, hence always one with it, in order that this great fact bear fruit in individual lives, each one must, as we have already said, be conscious of it; he must know it in thought, and then live continually in this consciousness. An eagle has been chained for many months to the perch just outside of his cage; so long has he been conscious of the fact that he is bound by the little silver chain which holds him that he has given up all efforts to escape, almost forgetting, perhaps, that the power of flight is longer his. One day a link of the little chain opens, but, living so long in the consciousness that he is held in captivity, he makes no effort to escape. The freedom of the heavens is now his, were he only conscious of his power. But day after day he sits sullenly longing for freedom but remaining a captive still. One morning, however, he ventures a little farther out on his perch than usual, when suddenly a strange consciousness is his—he sets his wings, and the captivity which has held him for months will perchance know him no more forever. And so it is with man. On account of the false gods that tradition and prevailing theology have brought him, he knows not himself, and not knowing himself he knows neither his powers nor his possibilities.

The human soul is held captive. An opaque physical structure is about all that he can be said truly to give evidence of. The day comes, however, when in his thought he moves out a little farther than is usual, then a little farther and a little farther. The Inner Light is now moving within, he catches at first a little glimpse of his real Essential Being, then a little more and a little more, and eventually the fact of his essential oneness with the Infinite Life and Power bursts in upon, illumines, and takes possession of his soul. In bewilderment, and almost afraid to utter it at first, he cries aloud, "O God, I am one with Thee!" Enraptured by this new consciousness, he holds to the thought of this oneness, and living continually in this thought his life forever after flows steadily on in one constant realisation of his oneness with Divine Being. And so "the first man, [which] is of the earth earthy," is changed into "the second man, [which] is the Lord from Heaven," and thereafter the Christ sits enthroned.

Compared with the new life that he is now continually living, the old life of ignorance with its consequent limitations, which can now know him no more forever, deserved only the name of death, for, in a sense, he was indeed dead unto life, and only he who lives in the conscious realisation of his oneness with the One and Only Life can be said truly to be born into Life. He is born into the world and lives in the world, but into consciously real and eternal Life he has not yet entered. He is born the Adam man, but within him the Christ man has not awakened, or, rather, he has not yet awakened to the Christ within, and so the Christ man is not yet born, and sitting therefore in darkness he knows not yet the glorious realities of life. "I am thine own Spirit" are the words that the Infinite Father by means of the Inner Voice is continually speaking to every human soul. He who will hear can hear, and through it step out into fulness of life.

We hear much in the prevailing crude and irrational theology in regard to the "fall of man;" but it is only as man has departed from the Inner Light, and gone after false man-made gods, that anything that might rationally be termed a "fall" has come about. Separating our lives in thought from their oneness with Divine Life is what constitutes, and what alone will ever constitute, the fall of man. But the teaching that has come to us through past generations, which has as its dominant keynote, poor worm and miserable sinner, death and the grave, is as false as it is pernicious and therefore damnable in its influences. These old thoughts and words have had the influence of taking heaven out of earth and populating the earth with doubt, and error, and sin, and crime. New and true thoughts and words will make literally a new heaven and a new earth.

Man is essentially Divine, part and parcel of the Infinite God, and so, essentially good. When he severs his connection in consciousness with the Divine, then and then only do doubt, and error, and sin, and crime, with their consequent pain, suffering, disease, and despair, enter into his life. Only a pure and radical infidel—by this we mean one who is in reality such, for there are many who are called infidels, even by many avowed religionists, who live a far truer religion than they themselves live—can rationally hold to the doctrine of original sin, with its consequent poor worm and miserable sinner. The religious teacher who professes to believe in God as the One Divine and Supreme Being and at the same time holds to this irrational doctrine, is many times more a disciple of the Devil, whom he recognises and whose power he evidently respects, than he is of the Infinite God in whom he professes to believe. He and he alone it is who finds a place for what he and his theology term the Devil. The one who truly believes in God as the only true and real being and the source of all life and power can indeed find no place for the Devil. He sees and recognises the evil that comes from lives that lose for a time their conscious connection with the Supreme Source of their being, but he can find no place for any other essential and abiding Reality.

And as this separation from God is made entirely through the instrumentality of the mind, he sees that making one's conscious connection again with God—the true and only true redemption—must also be made through the instrumentality of the mind. Believing in the God in whom he believes, and, knowing the God whom he knows, he sees no place for an atonement in the sense of appeasing the wrath of an angry God. Knowing the God whom he knows, he shares not in those barbaric, not to say idiotic, notions. He does see, however, that redemption can and must be through living in the conscious at-one-ment with the Father's life. He recognises it as the natural method that the Adam man be first born, with freedom of thought and consequently freedom of action, and that from him the Christ man then comes forth into consciousness. He recognises that it is God's, and consequently Nature's and evolution's method, that "the first man is of the earth earthy, the second man is the Lord from heaven." He recognises the fact that kittens are born blind, not because their parents or even their grand parents sinned, but because it is simply natural for them to be born blind, and that in process of time their eyes will open. He also recognises that, on account of our limited comprehension, the "natural" appears first and then the "spiritual," but in reality the spiritual is from the very first incarnated within, and only because it is can it in process of time, either sooner or later, assume the ascendancy by changing from potential into active life.

Once in a while there comes into the world one who from the very first recognises no separation of his life from the Father's life, and who dwells continually in this living realisation; and by bringing anew to the world this great fact, and showing forth the works that will always and inevitably follow this realisation, he becomes in a sense a world's saviour, as did Jesus, who, through the completeness of His realisation of the Father's life incarnate in Him, became the Christ Jesus. He in this way pointed out to the world how all men can enter into the realisation of the Christ-life and thus be saved from all impulse to sin. And so instead of coming to appease the vengeance of an angry God—difficult for one who has any adequate conception of God even to conceive of—He brought to the world, by exemplifying in His own life as well as by teaching to all who will hear His real message, the method whereby all of us can enter into the full and complete realisation of our oneness with the life of the tender and loving Infinite Father that dwells within.

Redeemed from the bondage of the senses through which alone sin comes, and born into the heavenly state, into life eternal, is everyone who comes into the same relations with the Father, and hence into the same realisation of their oneness with the Father's life, that Jesus came into. It is difficult, however, to see how anyone will be redeemed from the bondage of sin and enter into the heavenly state simply by believing that Jesus entered into it while here. No amount of believing that He lived the life He lived will take anyone into the heavenly state, but living the life that Jesus lived will take everyone who lives it there, in any age and in any time, even whether or not they know that such a man as Jesus ever lived.

The world has less need for a perverted and hence perverting doctrine of "vicarious atonement" that bodies of men have formulated by either intentionally or ignorantly dragging the teachings, as also the life, of the Master down to a purely material interpretation. Less need, most truly, has the world for this perverting doctrine than it has for the great vitalising fact of a conscious living at-one-ment with the Father's life, as everyone whose spiritual sense is at all unfolded will inevitably get from the life and teachings of the Master, if indeed they are more interested in the real living Truth that He taught than in the almost numberless man-made theological theories and dogmas regarding it.

In order that we may ever keep our standing ground clearly in mind, let us now gather into a single view the substance of what we have endeavoured thus far to present. From everlasting to everlasting is Being, self-existent, without beginning and without end. Depending upon nothing outside of Itself and the essential essence, the very life of all that through It comes into existence; It is therefore Infinite Being. Existing at first as pure Spirit, It is therefore Divine Being. Literally the "I Am," the Divine Jehovah, the Infinite God. Then, animated by love, and acting through Its own volition, It projects Itself into existence and assumes the various forms we see in the universe about us, including us ourselves. But by the act of projecting Itself into existence, the Infinite Divine Being does not change in the least Its essential inner nature, as indeed it would be impossible for it to do.

What, then, in reality is there in existence? Only Divine Being, the Infinite God in all His manifold manifestations; and thus it remains through all eternity, as must necessarily be from Its very nature, and otherwise It could not be. God, then, is the Infinite Being, the Infinite Spirit which is the essential essence, the Life of all, which therefore fills all the universe with Himself alone, so that all is He since He is all. But when Divine Being incarnates Itself in flesh and forms for Its use a physical body—a human body, as we call it—it necessarily has to manifest through the instrumentality of physical senses, and, though Divine Being is infinite, the vision of man is limited, and for a time his true inner Life (always Divine Being) is concealed from him, for he naturally interprets everything from the standpoint of the physical. First that which is natural, and man knows himself only as a natural physical being, differing not essentially from the material universe about him. As he looks out, however, he sees that he differs from other forms in existence, in that he has a mind through which thought is engendered, a mind that grows by using. Then contemplating himself and longing for the truth of his existence, gradually there dawns upon his consciousness the fact that his life is Divine Being, that other than this it has never been except in his own mind when in his thought he mistook the mere physical form in existence as the real essential life itself, thus separating his life from the Infinite Divine Life. He thus, realises that in God he lives, moves, and has his being, that God is the life of his life, his very life itself; and thus he comes in time into the conscious, living realisation of his oneness with the Infinite Life and Power. And so we find it true—first the natural man, then the spiritual.

Through thought, and through thought alone, the second man, the Lord from Heaven, is gradually evolved out of the first man, which is of the earth earthy. Through a perfectly natural process of evolution, out of the first man Adam—sense perception—is evolved the Christ- man—Divine self-realisation. Impossible, however, is it for anything to be evolved that was not first involved; and so man finds that the Lord Christ has always been within and he has known it not. It is the same today as it was many years ago with Jacob when he said, "Surely the Lord is in this place; and I knew it not." This and all that followed he found simply by using the stones of the place where he was; for with the stones of the place he made for himself a pillow, and it was while sleeping on this pillow that he beheld the ladder set upon the earth and reaching to the heavens, upon which the angels were ascending and descending, and thus it was that he entered into communion with the life of the heavens. Later, then, he transformed the pillow into a pillar that served as a guide to other men.

And so with every human soul—we must use simply the stones of the place where we are. The only stones with which human life can build is thought. It and it alone is the moulding, the creative power—earnest, sincere thought of the place where we are, this constitutes the stones of the place where we are and with which we can make a pillow upon which for the time being to rest. Through this and this alone will the life of the heavens be opened to us; for angels ascending —aspiration—will in time bring to us angels descending—inspiration. Then with Jacob of old we will cry out, "Behold, the Lord is in this place; and I knew it not." Then our pillow, the thought that gives us the knowledge that the Infinite Divine Life is always within, the Essential Essence of the human soul itself, we can convert into a pillar, a pillar that will be a guide to lead other men into this same realisation and life.

And so the entire problem of human life is wonderfully simple and easy if we are but true to the highest within us, and keep ourselves free from the various perplexing and mystifying theological theories and dogmas. These for the most part give merely a promise of spiritual awakening, realisation, and power in some other form of life, rather than actualising it here and now in this life. But only as man becomes conscious of the Lord Christ within, only as he becomes conscious— realises in thought that he is one with the Infinite Life and Power—does this great fact become a moving and mighty force in the affairs of his daily life. Until this is true he remains in the condition of the eagle, which, though unchained, thinking nevertheless that he was still chained, remained in captivity when the freedom of the heavens awaited simply the spreading of his wings.

Although the answer to our title has been given both in lines and between lines long before this, it may be an aid to us, especially in making practical what is to follow, to put it as best we can into a definite form: The greatest thing ever known— indeed, the greatest thing that ever can be known—is that in our real essential nature we are one with the Infinite Life and Power, and that by coming into, and dwelling continually in, the conscious, living realisation of this great fact, we enable to be manifested unto and actualised within us the qualities and powers of the Divine Life, and this in the exact degree of the completeness of this realisation on our part. The one great Truth of Being, therefore, is that there is no real Life except God (Good), and that the poor excuses for lives lived by so many today is simply the result of ignorance of this fact.

God is the Infinite Spirit of Life behind all, whence all comes, and our lives as individualised spirits are continually coming from this infinite Source by means of this divine inflow. As our lives as individualised spirits are directly from, are parts of the Infinite Spirit of Life, then the degree of the Infinite Spirit that is manifested in the life of each must be identical in quality with that Source, just as a drop of water taken from the ocean is, in nature, in characteristics, identical with the ocean, its source. And how could it be otherwise? The liability to misunderstanding, however, is this: in that although the Life of God and the life of man in essence are identically the same, the Life of God so far transcends the life of individual man that it includes all else beside. In other words, so far as the quality of life is concerned, in essence they are the same; so far as the degree of life is concerned they are vastly different. If it is true that there is no difference in essence but only in degree, does it not then follow that in the degree that man opens himself to this divine inflow does he approach to God? If so, it then necessarily follows that in the degree that he makes this approach does he take on the God-powers. And if the God-powers are without limit, does it not then follow that the only limitations man has are those he sets to himself, by virtue of not knowing himself and therefore not realising his innate possibilities?

Divine Energies in Everyday Life

Now what, let us ask, is the result and hence the value of this realisation? For unless it is of value in the affairs of everyday life, it is then a mere dead theory, and consequently of no real value. Use must be the final test of everything, and if it has no actual use, or if no visible results follow its use, we had better not spend time with it, for it is then not founded upon Truth.

First, let it be said, it is not the mere intellectual recognition, merely the dead theory, but the conscious vital and living realisation of this great truth, that makes it of value, and that makes it show forth in the affairs of everyday life. This it is, and this alone, that gives true blessedness, for this is none other than the finding of the kingdom of God, and when this is once found and lived in, all other things literally and necessarily follow. Through this the qualities and powers of the Divine Life are more and more realised and actualised, and through their leading we are led into the possession of all other things.

Those who come into this full and living realisation of oneness with the Divine Life are brought at once into right relations with themselves, with their fellow-man, and with the laws of the universe about them. They live now in the inner, the real life, and whatever is in the interior must necessarily take form in the exterior, for all life is from within out. There is no true life in regard to which this law does not hold. And if the will of God is done in the inward life, then is it necessarily done in all things of the outward life, and the results are always manifest. Thus and thus alone it is that individuals have become prophets, seers, and saviours; they have become what the world calls the "elect" of God, because in their own lives they first elected God and lived their lives in His life. And thus it is that today people can become prophets, seers, and saviours, for the laws of the Divine Life and the relations of what we term the human life to it are identically the same today as they have been in all time past and will be in all time to come.

The Divine Being changes not; it is man alone who changes. It is solely by virtue of man's leaving the inner life of the Spirit and thus departing from God, or by virtue of his not yet finding this real life, that sin and error, pain and disease, fears and forebodings, have crept as naturally and as necessarily as that effect follows cause into his life; only by closing his eyes to the inner light, by shutting his ears to the inner voice, that, although he has eyes to see, yet he sees not, and, although he has ears to hear, yet he hears not. It is only by uniting one's life with the Divine Life, and thus living again the life of the Spirit, that these things will go, even as they have come.

All the evil, unhappiness, misery, and want in the world are attributable to man, and are the direct results of his taking his life, either consciously or unconsciously, either directly or indirectly, out of harmony with the Power that works for righteousness and consequently for wholeness and perfection. And when our life is lived in the life of God, and God's will therefore becomes our will, all is and necessarily must be well with us, for contrary to His will it is impossible that anything should ever come to pass. And thus it is that he who seeks first the kingdom of God and His righteousness shall have all other things added unto him.

The soul, the real life, is Divine, and by allowing it to become translucent to Infinite Spirit by living continually in this conscious union with Divine Being it reveals all things to us. Things become hidden, mysteries fill and uncertainties pervade life only as we turn away from the inner light and life. There is nothing that is hidden of itself; to God all things are known, and one who consciously lives their life in the Life of God sees with the Divine vision that reveals all things to them. One who lives continually under this Divine guidance enters thereby into the realm of the highest wisdom, and even in the most trivial things of everyday life they never find themselves in a state of doubt or perplexity, for they always know what to do and how to do it. They have no regrets for the past, because before they entered into their present consciousness they were in a sense dead unto life, and all regrets that they might have for the past are now swallowed up in the joys that the new birth that has brought them into fulness of life continually spreads before their every step. They have neither fears nor forebodings in regard to the future, for they know that contrary to God's will, (which is now their will), nothing can ever come to pass. Peace, therefore, a full and abiding peace, is continually theirs.

As all life is from within out, and as this is absolutely true in regard to the physical body, the fountain of Divine Life that has been opened up within, which of itself can admit of no disease or imperfection of any kind, will allow only healthy conditions to be externalised in the body; and where unhealthy conditions have been built into it before entrance into the new life, the life that now courses through it will in time drive them out by entirely replacing the diseased structure with that which is pure and whole.

As you begin to grow in this realisation, a continually growing sense of power will be yours, for you are now working in conjunction with the Infinite God, and with God all things are possible. In material things you will not be lacking, for all things are from this one Infinite Source, and, guided by the Divine Wisdom and sustained by the Divine Power that are now yours; in a perfectly natural and normal way you find that an abundance of all things are yours, always at hand in sufficient time to supply all your material needs, and never is there lack when the time comes, if you simply do each day what your hands find to do. Sure always of this unfailing source of supply, one does not give oneself to the accumulation and the hoarding of great material possessions, thereby robbing life. Your thoughts will grow more and more into the nature of their Divine Source, and as thoughts are forces, and as in the degree that they are spiritualised do they become even more effective in their operations, so through their instrumentality you are able to mould more and more effectively the everyday conditions of life. And so as you enter into this new life you find that all things of the outer life fall into line; for as is the inner, so always and necessarily is the outer.

These truths will come as new revelations to many, and again to many they will come merely as agents to strengthen and possibly to arouse to renewed life the realisations of which they are already more or less conscious. In themselves, however, they are not new, but as old as the world. They are the real spirit of true Christianity; not, however, of the Christianity that the majority of people conventionally hold, and which in many respects is as radically inconsistent as it is void of results, but the great transcendent truths of our relations with the Father's life that Jesus taught. They are likewise the real essential spirit of all the great religions of the world, and as all religions in their purity are from the same source,—God speaking through the minds of those who have come into a sufficient union with Him to hear and to interpret His voice, the one universal source of all true inspiration and revelation,—so far as their fundamental principles are concerned they are necessarily the same.

The great spiritual awakening, the beginnings of which we are witnessing in all parts of the world today is evidence that the Divine Breath is stirring in the minds and hearts of men and women in a manner such as it has rarely if ever stirred before. Men and women are literally finding God. They are now breaking through the mere letter and form of an old and too-long-held ecclesiastical theorising and dogmatism into the real vital spirit of the religion of the living and transcendent God. They are waking here and there and everywhere to the realisation of their oneness with the living God. Their lives are being completely filled with this realisation, and as a consequence they are showing forth the works of God. They are leaving the old one-day-in-seven, some-otherworld religion, and they are finding the joys as well as the practicability of an everyday, this-world religion. They are passing out of the religion of death and possible glory hereafter into the religion of life and joy and glory here and now, today and everyday, as well as hereafter and forevermore.

With this new religion of the living God and the spiritual power that through it is being made active in their lives, they are moulding in detail all of the affairs of everyday life, proving thereby that their religion is the religion of life. And any system of religion that does not enable its possessor to do this is simply not religion; and we should no longer desecrate the Word by applying it to any such hollow mockeries. To this old semblance of religion those who are thus entering into this new and larger religion of life will never return, nor can they, anymore than the chick can enter within the confines of its shell again after it has been once born into life. Having found the pearl, the shell for them must perish; or rather, as it is of no farther value to them, it perishes simply by the operation of natural law. Centred thus in the Infinite, and working now in conscious harmony with Divine forces, they ever after rule the world from within.

The Master's Great but Lost Gift

The conclusions we have arrived at thus far we have arrived at independently of any authority outside of our own reason and insight. It is always of interest as well as of greater or less value to compare our own conclusions with those of others whose opinions we value. It would indeed be a matter of exceeding great interest to compare those we have reached with those of a number whose opinions come with greater or less authority to all the world. Space does not permit this, however, and I propose that we give the balance of our time to the consideration, though necessarily brief consideration, of two such; one universally regarded as one of the most highly illumined teachers, if not the most highly illumined, the world has ever known, the Christ Jesus; the other universally regarded as one of the most highly illumined philosophers the world has ever known, the philosopher Fichte. In these two we have the advantage of the life and teachings of one who lived and taught nearly nineteen hundred years ago, and one who lived and taught a trifle less than a hundred years ago. By selecting these, let it also be said, we have the advantage of two whose lives fully manifested the truth of that which they taught.

In considering the life and teachings of Jesus, let us consider them not as dull expositors interpret and represent them, but as He Himself gave them to the world. Certainly Jesus was Divine; but He was Divine, as He himself clearly taught, in just the same sense that you and I and every human soul is essentially Divine. He differed from us, however, in that He had come into a far clearer and fuller realisation of His divinity than we have come into, as indeed His life so clearly indicates. Jesus was God manifest in the flesh, as indeed every one must be who comes into the full realisation of their oneness with God, as Jesus Himself again so clearly taught.

In the thoroughly absurd, illogical, and positively demoralising doctrine of "vicarious atonement," as given us by early ecclesiastical bodies by perverting the real teachings of Jesus even to the extent of calling interpolations in the New Testament to their aid, we certainly cannot believe. Many do, however, believe that it has done more harm to the real teachings of Jesus, has been more productive of scepticism and infidelity, than all other causes combined. It is a doctrine that can be formulated only by those who have no spiritual insight themselves, and who therefore drag the teachings of the Master down to a purely material interpretation because of their inability to give them the spiritual interpretation that He intended they should have.

If Christ's mission was not that of vicarious atonement, not for the purpose of appeasing the wrath and indignation of an angry

God and thus reconciling Him to His children, what then was it? Clearly His mission was that of a Redeemer as He gave Himself out to be a Redeemer to bring the children of men back to their Father. And how did He purpose to do this? Clearly by having them consciously unite their lives with the Father's life, even as He had united his. The kingdom of God and His righteousness is not only what He came to teach, but what He clearly and unmistakably taught.

That He plainly and unequivocally taught His disciples that this was His mission is evidenced by numerous sentences such as the following, occurring all through the gospels: Matt. 4:23, "Jesus went about in all Galilee, teaching in their synagogues and preaching the gospel of the kingdom," etc. . .Luke 8:1, "He went about through cities and villages, preaching and bringing the good tidings of the kingdom of God". . . Luke 4:43, "But he said unto them: I must preach the good tidings of the kingdom of God to other cities also, for therefore was I sent." . . . Luke 9:2, "And he sent them forth to preach the kingdom of God and to heal the sick.". . . Matt. 24:14, "And this gospel of the kingdom shall be preached in the whole world, for a testimony unto all nations," etc. In more than thirty places in the first three gospels do we find Jesus thoroughly explaining to His disciples His especial mission—to preach the glad tidings of the coming of the kingdom of God; and even before He entered upon His public work, we hear John the Baptist going before Him and saying, "Repent ye; for the kingdom of Heaven is at hand."

What did Jesus mean by the kingdom of God, or, as He sometimes expressed it, the kingdom of Heaven? As an answer, and an answer better than any speculations in regard to it, let us again take His own words: "Neither shall they say, Lo here! or, Lo there! for, behold, the kingdom of God is within you." He taught only what He Himself had found, the conscious union with the Father's life as the one and all-inclusive thing. With Jesus from the very first, only in union with God was there reality. And this found, the conscious union with the life in the Father's life seemed nothing at all marvellous to Him; it was perfectly natural, and, the only life He knew. Hence He could not say otherwise than that He and the Father were one.

His vision was so clear and His already realised Divine life was so full and complete, that He knew that it was utterly impossible for His life to be without the Father's life, as we indeed shall know when our vision becomes clear and we enter into the same fully realised union with it. This great knowledge came to Jesus not through intellectual speculation and still less through any communication from without; it came to Him through His own interior consciousness; to all appearances He was born with it. He was born with a peculiar aptitude for discerning things of the Spirit, the same as among us some are born with a peculiar aptitude for one thing and others for other things. But so great was this power naturally in Jesus that in it we may justly say He had a great advantage over most people born into the world, and for this reason was He all the more able and all the greater reason was there for Him to be one of the great world Teachers and hence Redeemers.

He was indeed Immanuel—God with us. Jesus, I repeat, never speaks of His life in any other connection than as one with the Father's life. In reply to a question from Thomas in the fourteenth chapter of John, He says, "If ye had known me, ye would have known my Father also: from henceforth ye know Him and have seen Him not." Philip, who was standing near, unable to comprehend the interior meaning of the Master's words, said unto Him: "Lord, show us the Father, and it sufficeth us." Jesus, somewhat surprised that He had not made Himself clear to them, replied, "Have I been so long time with you, and dust thou not know me, Philip? He that hath seen me hath seen the Father; how sayest thou, Show us the Father? Believest thou not that I am in the Father, and the Father in me? The words I speak unto you I speak not from myself: but the Father abiding in me doeth His work. Believe me that I am in the Father and the Father in me: or believe me for the very works' sake."

But if His especial mission was to preach the good tidings of the kingdom of God, why, I hear it asked, did He claim that only through Him can we come unto the kingdom as He indeed says in His conversation with Philip and Thomas immediately preceding the part just quoted: "I am the way, the truth, and the life; no one cometh unto the Father but by me."? Yes He did, simply because it was the living Truth that He brought, which was and ever more is to redeem men by uniting them in mind and heart with the Father. He realised oneness with the Father's life was the way, the truth, and the life, and only by going over the same path that He

Himself had trod can anyone be truly united with the Father. He found this great, vital and redeeming truth nowhere else in the world; He had to speak as one standing alone, and in this sense He spoke most truly and most literally when He said, "No one cometh unto the Father but by me." And in order to point out His life, His realised oneness with the Father's life, as the way, the truth, and the life, He spoke and indeed had to speak as He did, even at the risk of being misunderstood and having His words taken in a purely material sense, as was the tendency of the spiritual poverty of the age, and indeed as His very disciples so often interpreted His words, as we have but recently seen.

In order to give forth the spiritual teachings which He gave, He had to use the language and the illustrations that their material minds could grasp, and in this way make His teachings doubly liable to a purely material interpretation. "I am the bread of life," said He to those assembled about Him; "your fathers did eat the manna in the wilderness, and they died. This is the bread which cometh down out of heaven, that a man may eat thereof, and not die. I am the living bread which came down out of heaven: if any man eat of this bread, he shall live forever: yea, and the bread which I will give is my flesh, for the life of the world." The Jews taking His words in a material sense argued one with another and said: "How can this man give us his flesh to eat?" Jesus simply reaffirmed His statement, saying: "Verily, verily, I say unto you, except ye eat the flesh of the son of man and drink his blood, ye have not life in yourselves. . . . For my flesh is meat indeed, and my blood is drink indeed." Literally, "My flesh is the true food, and my blood is the true drink. He that eateth my flesh and drinketh my blood abideth in me and I in him. As the living Father sent me, and I live because of the Father, so he that eateth me, he also shall live because of me." And many of His disciples, even when they heard Him speaking in this way, said among themselves, "This is a hard saying; who can hear him?"—who can understand him? Jesus, quickly perceiving that they were again dragging His words down to a material interpretation asked them if what He had just said caused them to stumble, and then, in order that they may get His real meaning, He said, "It is the spirit that quickeneth; the flesh profiteth nothing: the words that I have spoken unto you are spirit and are life."

And so all except those who are wholly spiritually, not to say even mentally, blind, can readily see that what Jesus meant to say, and what He actually did say, was, the words that He spoke to them of His oneness with the Father's life were the true meat and the true drink, of which, unless a man ate and drank, he had not life in himself, but that these were able to give him life and life eternal. "He that eateth my flesh and drinketh my blood abideth in me, and I in him." Or, reversing the expression, He that dwelleth in me and I in him, he it is that eateth my flesh and drinketh my blood. "The words that I have spoken unto you, (they) are spirit and (they) are life." "As the living Father hath sent me, and I live because of the Father, so he that eateth me, he also shall live because of me."

In the words of another, "To eat His flesh and drink His blood means to become wholly and entirely He Himself; to become altogether changed into His person without reserve or limitation; to be a faithful repetition of Him in another personality; to be transubstantiated with Him, i.e., as He is the Eternal Word made flesh and blood, to become His flesh and blood, and what follows from that, and indeed is the same thing, to become the very Eternal Word made flesh and blood itself; to think wholly and entirely like Him, and so as if He Himself thought and not we; to live wholly and entirely like Him, and so as if He Himself lived in our life.

"As surely as you do not now attempt to drag down my own words, and reduce them to the narrow meaning that Jesus is only to be imitated, as an unattainable pattern, partially and at a distance, as far as human weakness will allow, but accept them in the sense in which I have spoken them, that we must be transformed into Christ Himself, so surely will it become evident to you that Jesus could not well have expressed Himself otherwise, and that He actually did express Himself excellently well. Jesus was very far from representing Himself as that unattainable ideal into which He was first transformed by the spiritual poverty of the after-ages; nor did His apostles so regard Him." (quotation from Fichte in 'The Way towards the Blessed Life,')

To live in Christ is to live the life He lived, by living in the Truth in which He lived and which He taught. The one great Truth in which He continually lived was, as we have seen, that only in conscious union with God is there any real life, and therefore we can readily see why He continually gave out, as the gospel writers tell us so many times He did, that His especial mission was to preach the glad tidings of the kingdom of God. Were it not possible for us to live the same life that He lived, He certainly would not have taught what He taught. This wonderful life of fully realised Divine life Jesus claims not for Himself alone, but for all who actually live in the Truth that He taught. It was not to establish any material institution, as the church, that Jesus made His mission, but that the kingdom of God and His righteousness should become actualised and hold sway in the minds and hearts of men—this was His mission, an entirely different thing from the founding of a material organisation.

Paul and his party, sharing the then prevailing ideas that a material kingdom was to be established, were the originators of the church, not Jesus. We find the word 'church' mentioned in the four Gospels by Jesus only once or twice, and then only in an incidental way, while we find the kingdom mentioned over thirty times in the first three Gospels alone. As we have already pointed out, had it been His purpose to establish a material organisation, then He certainly would not have given it out that something else was His especial purpose. But when the material organisation, the church, purely a man-made institution, was established, the early church fathers bringing even interpolations of the Holy Word to their aid in establishing it and some of its various observations,— as modern scholarship has already so clearly discovered, and as it is continually discovering,—the following ages, thinking that they had an institution to keep up, gradually lost, to a greater or less extent, the real spiritual teachings of the Master in their zeal to keep up the form of an institution with which He had nothing to do. And those long and bitter persecutions of the church in the early and middle ages, as well as the long list of crimes sanctioned and committed directly by the church of the middle ages, show that they had not the real truth; for those who live in the truth and have it uppermost in their minds and hearts never persecute—only those who are on either uncertain or false ground, and whose endeavour it is to keep up the form of an institution which they feel would otherwise fall to the ground.

No, true religion has never been known either to persecute or to show intolerance of any kind. Throughout the whole history of the churches' heresies and persecutions, the persecuted party has ever occupied a correspondingly higher and the persecuting party a lower position, the persecuting party continually fighting as it were for life. But the Real Truth that Jesus taught will not cause nor will it even permit persecutions—hence we find the latter only where there is the lack of the former. And again, the Real Truth that Jesus taught will not admit of divisions, much less of intolerance, for all real truth is exact truth, and in regard to it there can be no differences, and our modern theologians, and our churches of today, which get their form and life from the speculations and theories of the former, certainly have not the real Truth that Jesus taught for they are divided in various directions on practically every dogma that they seek to promulgate.

And strange as it may seem, heresy trials, with all their absurd attendant features, are not entirely unknown even yet today. But in Jesus' own words, "A house divided against itself cannot stand." And so if the church of today wants to stand as a real power in the world, or if indeed it wants to stand at all, it must either get back to, or it must come up, as the case may be, to the real Living Truth that Jesus lived and taught. Unless it does this it will inevitably lose its hold on the people even more rapidly than it is losing it today. And certainly the younger ones whom it does not yet hold will not be drawn to it, when they can turn to that which has a thousand-fold more of truth and hence of life-giving power than it has to offer.

That this is not a mere sentiment on our part is evidenced by the wonderful rapidity with which the "New Thought" movement—would that we could designate what we mean without using any term—which has its underlying Truth, this conscious union with the Divine Life and the actualised powers attendant upon it as Jesus taught,—hence not a new discovery, but a recovery,—is growing in America, in England, to be brief, in practically every civilised country in the world. Thousands every year in our own and in other countries are finding in it the joys of the realised Divine Life, and are turning to it from that which but poorly feeds them; and that this also is no mere sentiment on our part is evidenced by the contents of a letter recently sent by a noted divine in high official standing in the church in England to a noted American preacher, in which he said, in substance, that the church in England is literally honey-combed by the "New Thought" movement, and asked that he be sent a list of the best books that had already appeared in America along the lines indicated.

And so what we need today is the same as what the world is eagerly calling for, the life-giving power of the great central Truth that the Master taught, and not the various theories and speculations in regard to His origin, His birth, His life, and the meaning of His teachings. And still less, the fabrications of the early church fathers in regard to inherited sin, original sin, vicarious atonement, and their believe-and- be-saved doctrine, and the alternative doctrine—fail to believe that which is opposed to all reason, all common sense, all real mercy, as well as all true justice, and be damned, be forever and eternally lost.

Jesus is indeed a lamb of God that taketh away the sins of the world, but He takes them away by bringing to the world the Truth that shall make men free. Hence it is through His life and the Truth that He lived and taught, not through His death and the observance of the various ceremonies and forms that have grown up around it. Those who are aided by symbols—and I am aware of the fact that for some, many hallowed associations are connected with them—may do well to make use of them until they outgrow the need for them. But symbols are of value only where the real thing is not, and those who have the real thing no longer have need for symbols. "But the hour cometh," said Jesus, "and now is" (since I have brought you the real Spirit of Truth), "when the true worshippers shall worship the Father in spirit and truth; for such doth the Father seek to be His worshippers. God is Spirit, and they that worship Him must worship in spirit and truth."

Jesus, according to His own words, did not propose to rest satisfied with the mere historical belief that He was the Eternal Word made flesh, and much less, as some phases of theology teach, that reconciliation with the Father, as ordinarily understood, was His purpose. God would adopt no methods in connection with His children that are opposed to their own reason. Nor would He adopt any partial, limited, or tribal methods. And if, as various theologians would have us believe, that reconciliation with the Father can come about only by a belief in the shedding of the material physical blood of Jesus, that through it the Father may receive satisfaction for His favour, how, then, in regard to the great company of those who cannot accept a theory so absurd, so illogical, and so opposed to the nature of the living God whom they know, and whom they no longer have to speculate and theorise in regard to, to say nothing of the millions upon millions of those who never have heard, and other millions who never can hear, of the man Jesus and the story of His blood "shed for the sins of the world," nine-tenths of whom, for good reasons, would not believe it if they did hear it?

No, these fabrications cannot be true, for "in every nation, he that feareth God and worketh righteousness is accepted of Him." And so one may be without connection with any church, and even without connection with any established religion, and yet be in spirit, hence in reality, a much truer Christian than hosts of those who profess to be His most ardent followers, as indeed Jesus Himself so many times says. "By their fruits ye shall know them," said He. "Not every one that saith unto me, Lord, Lord, shall enter into the kingdom of heaven; but he that doeth the will of my Father which is in heaven."

That which calls itself Christianity must prove itself, and only that that shows forth in its life the works, the power, the influence—the Truth that Jesus' life showed forth—is the real. "He that believeth on me," said Jesus,—and shows it by living my life,—"the works that I do shall he do also; and greater works than these shall he do because I go unto the Father." And he who would know by what authority Jesus spoke, let him live the life that He lived and he will then know of the doctrine. Thus and thus only can it be known. We may speculate and theorise in regard to it, but only by living the life can we know it.

The Philosopher's Ripest Life Thought

Let us now see how the truths we have already set forth stand in reference to the thought of the philosopher Fichte. Truth, the highest truth, and truth for its own sake, was the one supreme object of his life. And in order to discern this clearly himself, that he in turn might point it out clearly to others, he stood erect and alone, free from connection with any institution, organisation, or system of thought that would distort or limit his vision and induce him either intentionally or unintentionally to interpret truth by bending it to suit the tenets of the system of thought or the institution to which he might be, even though inadvertently, bound.

It was of Fichte that an eminent English scholar once said: "Far above the dark vortex of theological strife in which punier intellects chafe and vex themselves in vain, Fichte struggles forward in the sunshine of pure thought which sectarianism cannot see, because its weakened vision is already filled with a borrowed and imperfect light."

It is, moreover, always of value to know how the truth that one finds and endeavours to give to others finds embodiment in his own life, for this is the sure and unfailing test of its vitality, if not indeed of its reality. A word or two, therefore, in reference to the life of Fichte may not be inappropriate here, a word or two from the same eminent English scholar quoted above, the translator of his works from the German to the English, for he knew well his life the same as he knew also his philosophy. "We prize his philosophy deeply," says he; "it is to us an invaluable possession, for it seems the noblest exposition to which we have yet listened of human nature and divine truth; but with reverent thankfulness we acknowledge a still higher debt, for he has left behind him the best gift which man can bequeath to man—a brave, heroic human life." "In the strong reality of his life,—in his intense love for all things beautiful and true,—in his incorruptible integrity and heroic devotion to the right, we see a living manifestation of his principles. His life is the true counterpart of his philosophy—it is that of a strong, free, incorruptible man."

And now to a few paragraphs of Fichte's thought bearing more or less directly upon the theme immediately in hand. After setting forth in a very comprehensive manner the truth in regard to Being, which he identifies with Life much in the same general manner as we have already endeavoured to set it forth, and then after making it clear that by God he means this Infinite Being, this Spirit of Infinite Life, he says: "God alone is, and nothing besides him,—a principle which, it seems to me, may be easily comprehended, and which is the indispensable condition of all religious insight." "But beyond this mere empty and imaginary conception, and as we have carefully set forth this matter above, God enters into us in His actual, true, and immediate life,—or, to express it more strictly, we ourselves are this His immediate Life. But we are not conscious of this immediate Divine Life; and since, as we have also already seen, our own Existence—that which properly belongs to us—is that only which we can embrace in consciousness, so our Being in

God, notwithstanding that at bottom it is indeed ours, remains nevertheless forever foreign to us, and thus, in deed and truth, to ourselves is not our Being; we are in no respect the better of this insight, and remain as far removed as ever from God."

"We know nothing of this immediate Divine Life, I said; for even at the first touch of consciousness it is changed into a dead World. . . . The form forever veils the substance from us; our vision itself conceals its object; our eye stands in its own light. I say unto thee who thus complainest: 'Raise thyself to the standing-point of Religion, and all these veils are drawn aside; the World, with its dead principle, disappears from before thee, and the Godhead once more resumes its place within thee, in its first and original form, as Life,—as thine own Life, which thou oughtest to live and shalt live.'"

In setting forth how universally Divine Being incarnates itself in human Life, he says: "From the first standing-point the Eternal Word becomes flesh, assumes personal, sensible, and human existence, without obstruction or reserve, in all times, and in every individual man who has a living insight into his unity with God, and who actually and in truth gives up his personal life to the Divine Life within him,—precisely in the same way as it became incarnate in Jesus Christ."

Speaking, then, of the great fundamental fact of the Truth that Jesus Himself perceived and gave to the world, and also of the manner whereby He came into the perception of it, he says: "Jesus of Nazareth undoubtedly possessed the highest perception containing the foundation of all other truth, of the absolute identity of Humanity with the Godhead, as regards what is essentially real in the former." "His self-consciousness was at once the pure and absolute Truth of Reason itself, self-existent and independent, the simple fact of consciousness." Then in showing that Jesus as He is presented to us by the apostle John never conceived of His life in any other light than as one with the Father's Life, he says: "But it is precisely the most prominent and striking trait in the character of the Johannean Jesus, ever recurring in the same shape, that He will know nothing of such a separation of His personality from His Father, and that He earnestly rebukes others who attempt to make such a distinction; while He constantly assumes that he who sees Him sees the Father, that he who hears Him hears the Father, and that He and the Father are wholly one; and He unconditionally denies and rejects the notion of an independent being in Himself, such an unbecoming elevation of Himself having been made an objection against Him by misunderstanding. To Him Jesus was not God, for to Him there was no independent Jesus whatever; but God was Jesus, and manifested Himself as Jesus."

To show, then, that this is a universal truth, brought in its fulness, and with a living exemplified vitality, first to the world by Jesus, but by no means applicable to Him alone, he says: "An insight into the absolute unity of the Human Existence with the Divine is certainly the profoundest Knowledge that man can attain. Before Jesus this Knowledge had nowhere existed; and since His time, we may say, even down to the present day, it has been again as good as rooted out and lost, at least in profane literature."

That we must come into the same living realisation of this great, transcendent Truth that Jesus came into, either through His teaching and exemplified realisation of it, or through whatever channel it may come, he clearly indicates by the following: "The living possession of the theory we have now set forth—not the dry, dead, and merely historical knowledge of it—is, according to our doctrine, the highest, and indeed the only possible, Blessedness." "The Metaphysical only, and not the Historical, can give us Blessedness; the latter can only give us understanding. If any man be truly united with God, and dwell in Him, it is altogether an indifferent thing how he may have reached this state; and it would be a most useless and perverse employment, instead of living in the thing, to be continually repeating over our recollections of the way. Could Jesus return into the world, we might expect Him to be thoroughly satisfied, if He found Christianity actually reigning in the minds of men, whether His merit in the work were recognised or overlooked; and this is, in fact, the very least that might be expected from a man who, while He lived on earth, sought not His own glory, but the glory of God who sent Him."

And what in the eyes of Fichte are the results that follow and hence the tests of the genuineness of this higher realisation, this True Religion, as he sometimes terms it? His words in this connection are: "True Religion, notwithstanding that it raises the view of those who are inspired by it to its own region, nevertheless retains their Life firmly in the domain of action, and of right moral action. The true and real Religious Life is not alone percipient and contemplative, does not merely brood over devout thoughts, but is essentially active. It consists, as we have seen, in the intimate consciousness that God actually lives, moves, and perfects His work in us. If therefore there is in us no real Life, if no activity and no visible work proceed forth from us, then is God not active in us. Our consciousness of union with God is then deceptive and vain, and the empty shadow of a condition that is not ours; perhaps the general, but lifeless, insight that such a condition is possible, and in others may be actual, but that we ourselves have, nevertheless, not the least portion in it."

"Religion does not consist in mere devout dreams, I said: Religion is not a business by and for itself, which a man may practice apart from his other occupations, perhaps on certain fixed days and hours; but it is the inmost spirit that penetrates, inspires, and pervades all our Thought and Action, which in other respects pursue their appointed course without change or interruption. That the Divine Life and Energy actually lives in us is inseparable from Religion, I said."

To show, then, how completely at one in his or her consciousness this truly religious man or woman becomes, how his or her own personal will is lost in, and so transmuted into, the Divine Will, as also the calmness and tranquillity with which his or her life forever thereafter flows along, he says: "The expression of the constant mind of the truly Moral and Religious man is this prayer: 'Lord! let but thy will be done, then is mine also done; for I have no other will than this—that thy will be done."

"This Divine Life now continually develops itself within him, without hindrance or obstruction, as it can and must develop itself only in him and his individuality; this alone it is that he properly wills; his will is therefore always accomplished, and it is absolutely impossible that anything contrary to it should ever come to pass."
"Whatever comes to pass around him, nothing appears to him strange or unaccountable—he knows assuredly, whether he understand it or not, that it is in God's World, and that there nothing can be that does not directly tend to Good. In him there is no fear for the future, for the absolute fountain of all Blessedness eternally beats him on towards it; no sorrow for the past, for in so far as he was not in God he was nothing, and this is now at an end, and since he has dwelt in God he has been born into Light; while

in so far as he was in God, that which he has done is assuredly right and good. He has never aught to deny himself, nor aught to long for; for he is at all times in eternal possession of the fulness of all that he is capable of enjoying. For him all labour and effort have vanished; his whole Outward Existence flows forth, softly and gently, from his Inward Being, and issues out into Reality without difficulty or hindrance."

Speaking, then, of how we may at once enter into and live in the full realisation of this real life, and also of those who, instead of entering immediately into the Kingdom and thus finding the highest happiness and joy here and now, are expecting to find it in its completeness after the transition we call death, he says: "Full surely indeed there lies a Blessedness beyond the grave for those who have already entered upon it here, and in no other form or way than that by which they can already enter upon it here in this moment; but by mere burial man cannot arrive at Blessedness—and in the future life, and throughout the whole infinite range of all future life, they would seek for happiness as vainly as they have already sought it here, if they were to seek it in aught else but that which already surrounds them so closely here below that throughout Eternity it can never be brought nearer to them in the Infinite. And thus does the poor child of Eternity, cast forth from his native home, and surrounded all sides by his heavenly inheritance which yet his trembling hand fears to grasp, wander with fugitive and uncertain step throughout the waste, everywhere labouring to establish for himself a dwelling place but happily ever reminded, by the speedy downfall of each of his successive habitations, that he can find peace nowhere but in his Father's house."

Finally, speaking of how completely doubt and uncertainty are eliminated from the life of him who through the realisation of the Truth we have set forth becomes thereby centred in the Infinite, he says: "The Religious man is forever secured from the possibility of doubt and uncertainty. In every moment he knows distinctly what he wills, and ought to will; for the innermost root of his life—his will—forever flows forth from the Divinity, immediately and without the possibility of error; its indication is infallible, and for that indication he has an infallible perception. In every moment he knows that in all Eternity he shall know what he shall will, and ought to will; that in all Eternity the fountain of Divine Love which has burst forth in him shall never be dried up, but shall uphold him securely and bear him on forever"

Such, then, in general, are fragments of the thought, and, let it be added, the ripest thought, of one who has exerted perhaps as great a direct influence upon the life of his own immediate as well as succeeding ages as any man who has lived in modern times. It is to Fichte that, to a very great extent, Germany owes the splendid educational system it has today. His thought began to exert its influence at the time when the country's educational system was falling into a state of chaos, and, acting to a greater or less extent through the minds of Froebel and Pestalozzi, his thought has aided in giving to the world one of the truest systems of education it has yet seen. If the truth and vitality of a man's thought are to be judged by its permanent as well as its immediate influence, surely the thought of Fichte found its life in the realms of the highest Truth, through which alone real vitality comes, for it has exerted and is still exerting a most powerful life-giving influence, an influence, indeed, that will never end.

Sustained in Peace and Safety Forever

At what now have we arrived, and what has been the process? From our own reason and insight, independently of all outside authority, we have found the great truth that a living insight into the fact of the essential unity of the human life with the Divine Life is the profoundest knowledge that man can attain to. This as a mere intellectual perception, however, as a mere dead theory, amounts to but little, if indeed to anything at all, so far as bearing fruit in everyday life is concerned. It is the vital, living realisation of this great transcendent truth in the life of each one that makes it a mighty moving and moulding force in their life.

Then we have also found that this same great Truth was the great central fact of both the life and the teachings of one who comes as authority to practically all the world, the Christ Jesus. That this was the one great Truth in which He continually lived, that it was the secret of His unusual insight and power, and that it was also the great Truth that He came to bring to the world, He distinctly tells us. That it was not only what He proclaimed He came to teach, but also what He distinctly taught, we have likewise found.

We have found also that the ripest life thought of the philosopher Fichte—he whose spiritual vision was so fully unfolded as to enable him to give to the world such a remarkable blending of the intellectual and the spiritual in his philosophy—was almost if not identically the same in reference to this great Truth, as was also his thought in regard to the life and the power as well as the mission of Jesus. And when I see day after day the wonderful results that follow in the lives of those who have entered into this living realisation, then I know that Jesus knew whereof He spoke when He gave the injunction, "Seek ye first the kingdom of God and His righteousness and all these things shall be added unto you." Moreover I do not believe, but I know, that whoever through this realisation thus finds the kingdom of God will find His words—that all else will follow—literally and absolutely as well its necessarily true.All will follow in a perfectly natural and normal manner, in full accordance with natural spiritual law.

He who goes thus directly to the mountain top will find all things spread out before him in the valley below. He who thus becomes centred in the Infinite will find that to the same centre whence his inner life issues, all things pertaining to his outer material life will in turn be drawn.

The beauty of holiness is one with the beauty of wholeness. To know but the One Life is to live in the fact and the beauty of wholeness; and where wholeness is, there no lack of anything will be found. Also, if what we ordinarily term our Christian churches, and if the preachers who stand in their pulpits would fully and universally give themselves to the real message that Jesus gave to the world, then we would find that "the common people" would go to and would hear them gladly; there would then be no hard pressing social situation to face, for the people would then have a living knowledge of the one great Truth through which all other things would come.

This great transcendent Truth, however, that was the very essence of the life and the teachings of Jesus, has been even in our churches as good as rooted out and lost. And shall we conclude that because it is practically lost, the greater part of the time and attention of the preacher in the large majority of them is given to the empty, barren, inconsequential themes it is given to? Or is it because so much time and attention is given to the latter that there is no time left for the former? However this may be, it certainly is true that to a greater or less extent today we find identically the same conditions that Jesus found, and that He continually tried so hard to do away with. "Full well," said He, "ye reject the commandment of God, that ye may keep your own tradition."

Many a student comes from our theological schools so steeped in theological speculations and in denominational dogmas that he hasn't the slightest conception of what the real mission of Jesus was. What wonder, then, that the church to which he goes soon becomes a dead shell from which the life has gone, into which those in love with life will no longer enter, a church whose chief concern very soon is, how to raise the minister's salary? But once let these minor and inconsequential, not to say at times petty, foolish, and absurd, things be dropped, and let all time and attention be given to the great central Truth that Jesus brought to he world, and we shall find that during the next one hundred years, or maybe during the next fifty years, what will then be real Christianity will make more progress than what is now termed Christianity has made during all the nineteen hundred years it has been in the world.

The fact that during all these hundreds of years it has not accomplished more than it has is quite good evidence that something essential is lacking in it. The real soul-cry even of all Christendom today is the same as the injunction given by the native ministers of Japan to a noted representative of the Christian religion as he was leaving there not long ago: "Send us no more doctrines: we are tired of them. Send us Christ." And the only way that Christ can be sent is by sending the great central Truth that He brought to the world, a truth so world-wide, so universal, that, so far even as the so-called various great religions are concerned, in regard to it there can be no differences, for from its very nature it is at the very foundation, indeed, the very life essence, of them all.

And so it is true in this sense that there is essentially but one religion, the religion of the living God. For to live in the conscious realisation of the fact that God lives in us, is indeed the life of our life, and that in ourselves we have no independent life, and hence no power, is the one great fact of all true religion, even as it is the one great fact of human life. Religion, therefore; at its purest, and life at its truest, are essentially and necessarily one and the same.

It is only through this living realisation of the essential unity of our life with the Father's life that true blessedness, and even true peace and happiness, can be found. The sooner, then, that we come into it, and thus live the life of the spirit, the better, for neither will they come nor can they be found in any other way. There is, moreover, no time either in this form of life, or in any other form, that we can any more readily come into it, and thereby into all that follows, than we can at this very moment. And when this fountain of Divine Life is once fully opened within us, it can never again be dried up, and we can rest assured that it will at all times uphold us in peace and bear us on in safety. And however strange or unaccountable at times occurrences may appear, we can rest in a triumphant security, knowing that only good can come, for in God's life there is only good, and in God's life we are now living, and there we shall live forever.

There is a simple method which will aid us greatly in coming into the realisation we have been considering, So simple is it that thousands and indeed millions have passed it by, looking, as is so generally our custom, for agencies of at least apparently greater power; we so frequently and so universally forget that the greatest things in life are the most simple. The method is this: wherever you are, whatever doing, walking along the street or through the fields, at work of any kind, falling off to or awaking from sleep, setting about any undertaking, in doubt as to what course to pursue at any particular time, in brief, whatever it may be, carry with you this thought: It is the Father that worketh in me, my Father works and I work. This is the thought so continually used by Jesus, who came into probably the fullest realisation of the oneness of His life with the God-life that anyone who has lived in the world thus far has come into, and it is given because it is so simple.

From it each can make his own formula. Jesus' term was "the Father." Many will likewise find themselves naturally using the same term and will find it becoming very precious to them. Others will find themselves using other terms for the same conception and thought: It is the Father that worketh in me, my Father works and I work. In other words, It is the Spirit of Infinite Life and Power that is back of all, working in and through all, the life and animating power of all,—God,—that worketh in me, and I do as I am directed and empowered by It. In this way we open ourselves, and become consciously awake to the Infinite Life and Power that is ever waiting and ready to direct and work in our lives, if we will merely put ourselves into the attitude whereby It can work in them. In this way we open ourselves so that It can speak and manifest to and through us. This It is ever ready to do if we will but make for It the right conditions.

By carrying with us this thought, by holding ourselves in this attitude of mind consciously for awhile, by repeating it even in so many words now and then at first, we will find it in time becoming our habitual thought, and will find ourselves living in it without the conscious effort that we have to make at first, and we will in time find ourselves almost unconsciously living in it continually. Thus God as a living presence, as a guiding, animating power, becomes an actuality in our lives.

The conscious presence of God in our lives, which is the essence, indeed the sum and substance of all religion, then becomes a reality, and all wisdom and all power will be given us as we are able to appropriate and use them wisely; if for merely selfish, personal ends, they will be withheld; if for the greatest aid and service for the world, we will find them continually increasing. With this higher realisation comes more and more the simple, child-like spirit. With Jesus we realise—Of myself I can do nothing, it is the Father within me that doeth His work. In ourselves we are and can do nothing; in God we can do all things.

We never can be in the condition—in God—until through this higher realisation God becomes a conscious, living reality in our lives. Faithfulness to this simple method will bring about a complete change in great numbers of lives. Each one for themselves can test its efficacy in a very short time. It is the highway upon which many will enter that will by easy stages take them into the realisation of the highest life that can be attained to. To set one's face in the right direction, and then simply to travel on, will in time bring one into the realisation of the highest life that can be even conceived of—it is the secret of all attainment.

www.ingramcontent.com/pod-product-compliance
Lightning Source LLC
Chambersburg PA
CBHW031655040426
42453CB00006B/317